FROM HARD KNOCKS
TO HOT STOCKS

FROM
HARD KNOCKS
TO HOT STOCKS

How I Made a Fortune Through Smart
Investing and How You Can Too

J. MORTON DAVIS

William Morrow and Company, Inc. New York

It is the policy of William Morrow and Company, Inc., and its imprints and affiliates, recognizing the importance of preserving what has been written, to print the books we publish on acid-free paper, and we exert our best efforts to that end.

Library of Congress Cataloging-in-Publication Data

Davis, J. Morton.
From hard knocks to hot stocks : how I made a fortune through smart investing and how you can too / J. Morton Davis.
p.   cm.
Includes index.
ISBN 0-688-15322-4
1. Stocks—United States. 2. Going public (Securities)—United States. I. Title.
HG4963.D384 1998
332.63'22—dc21   97-27352
                                                                        CIP

Printed in the United States of America

First Edition

1   2   3   4   5   6   7   8   9   10

www.williammorrow.com

To my gorgeous, vivacious, and brilliant wife, Rozi,
with whom I made my greatest merger;

Our best dividends—our beautiful and bright daughters,
Esti, Ruki, Rivki, and Laya;

Their outstanding husbands, Ushi Stahler, Kal Renov, Lindsay
Rosenwald, and Dov Perlysky;

And our newest issues—our fantastic grandchildren.
They are blue chips one and all.

VI.

FOREWORD

People will tell you that the American dream is dead—or, if not dead, at least badly tarnished. Rags to riches was yesterday's news, they insist; today you need Ivy League parents, an M.B.A., a corporate "team player" approach. The hero who emerges from poverty to build a better life for others is a musty legend, lost in another century. If he were somehow, improbably, to surface in today's world, the one place you could be certain not to find him would, of course, be Wall Street.

The skeptics never met J. Morton Davis.

Morty might just as easily have become the bum he is convinced his father expected him to be. Growing up as a poor, Depression-era kid on the mean streets of Brooklyn's Williamsburg, the hooky-playing youth was so far from being any kind of "intellectual" that his only discernible ambition was eventually to find an indoor job. The tale of how, belatedly, he found himself, buckled down, and built a career, a fortune—and a life—is the gritty stuff of true inspiration. One is tempted to use the phrase "only in America," but Davis's saga is broader than that; it is the sort of amazing self-help story that helps us understand why the American dream, so long disparaged even within our own borders, has now so thrillingly become the world's dream.

For Morty Davis's story is not just poor-boy-makes-good—not even poor-boy-makes-millions. Our infatuation with those extraordinary numbers is only a fraction of this saga. Morty's fortune was built in the purest realm of capitalism and his success is thus doubly unfashionable. Capitalism is supposed to be a dirty word and its winners are fair game for every sharpshooter from the classrooms to the Congress.

Yet, in truth, Morty Davis's activities should be seen as downright romantic. He is a premier underwriter of new stock issues, which means quite simply that his firm helps make it possible for people with more ideas than dollars to realize their dreams. His success in spotting promising small companies, in a variety of fields, is legendary. The way a firm like his nurtures and mentors such fledgling operations may be as close as a man can come to being a mother. Such investments by their nature involve high risks; even a record as dazzling as Morty's shows disappointments, wounds, and heartbreaks.

Morty understands and identifies with the imaginative entrepreneurs who are the keys to any nation's authentic future. But a significant part of Morty's genius, as he recounts it in *From Hard Knocks to Hot Stocks*, is his ability to identify as well with those who are sought as investors in these projects by routinely pricing his initial offers below the prevailing market multiples, thus increasing the chances of profits for all concerned.

The beauty of this book is that it so vividly conveys the flavor of the man: the outpouring of anecdotes, opinions, and unstuffy revelations. His former professors at Harvard Business School should be proud of his presentation of "case studies" that illustrate his theories as to how we can all do as well as he. Those who yearn to emulate such success should observe carefully how hard this man continues to work, how strong—he would say "neurotic"—is his ongoing drive, how profound his commitment to the job, not just the bucks. Envy is a pernicious human emotion, and the superficial will always be looking for the angle, the flaw, the evidence that "luck" was all that really mattered. Those who actually want to learn something, on the other hand, will find a lot to learn in this book.

There's something else about Morty that will, I think, come through to those who read this remarkable book; he is what my late mother used to call "a builder-upper, not a tearer-downer." This is obviously true in his professional activities, which contrast so plainly with those of the corporate raiders and the merchants of computer-driven hysteria for mindless institutional traders. But it is also conspicuous in his personal life. He is constantly praising others—a rare talent in this egocentric era. As I sat one day in his elegant, old-world Wall Street office—so close geographically to Williamsburg, so far in every other way—listening to the endless flow of his self-deprecating tales, we were interrupted by a member of his staff who needed advice regarding a business decision. Before giving his opinion, Morty stopped to recite for me this individual's life story, which seemed to Morty to be only a trifle less heroic than that of Joan of Arc.

Morty Davis is genuinely enchanted with people and how people can succeed in business. In the pages that follow, the enchantment is contagious.

—LOUIS RUKEYSER

copyright 7/1998

ACKNOWLEDGMENTS (typescript)

by J. Morton Davis

I knew when I finished the first draft of this book that it needed the added insights of two of the best experts on my life story and investment philosophy. So, despite the fact that they were already busy raising sixteen (they have eight each) of my (twenty-three and counting) grandchildren, I turned to my daughters Esti and Ruki, who spent many long hours helping me put a lifetime of strategies, investment philosophies, and anecdotes on paper. They did a super job, and I'm very proud of them.

In addition, major contributions, insights, and editing also came from my priceless son-in-law, Kal Renov. I must also thank my ever-wise counsel Marty Bell and my dedicated assistants, Alison Brown, Karin Coakley, and Debbie Cook.

My thanks as well to Bob Andelman and Laurie Blancher, who assisted in the final preparation of the book.

There is no way I can adequately show my deep appreciation and love to my very special partner in life, Rozi. I told her that it would take a thousand pages just to begin to express my love and admiration for her as an incomparable wife and mother and a beautiful and delightful person. She said, "Well, just start writing."

Finally, I would like to thank my entire family. Without their constantly reminding me of more stories to include and continuously encouraging me to keep writing, I might have been done with this book years ago.

CONTENTS

No Glossary...

XIV

INTRODUCTION

goes to pg XXIII = 9 pgs

A wealthy man invited all his friends to see his beautiful Florida home and magnificent estate. When they arrived he showed them his lake full of ferocious alligators. "Because I prize courage above all else," he told the crowd, "anyone who will swim across the lake can have anything he wants: my luxurious home, my exquisite yacht, or my multimillion-dollar bank account." All of the guests took one look at the lake full of ferocious man-eating reptiles, turned incredulously, and walked away.

Suddenly, a voice in the crowd shouted, "Look! Someone is trying it!" Everyone turned around to see one of the guests swimming like a madman, racing, splashing, thrashing through the water with an alligator only a stroke behind.

Miraculously, he made it.

The guests were stunned. The wealthy owner was flabbergasted, but he approached, patted the swimmer on the back, and said, "I never dreamed anyone would have the bravado to try it, but I am a man of my word. You can have anything you want. Just name it."

Dripping, breathless, and wild-eyed, the swimmer looked up at his host and said, "What do I want? What do I want? I want the wise guy who pushed me into that lake!"

That's what I sometimes feel like asking: Who in the world pushed me into Wall Street, the world's most treacherous man-eating lake?

This book describes what I learned during years of struggling to keep my head above water. I came in with the Crash of 1929, born to poor immigrant parents in the Williamsburg section of Brooklyn, the first of three children. We were so poor that when they collected for charity at school, I thought it was for me.

Instead of going to school in the morning, I rode the subway up to the Paramount Theatre at Times Square and caught a movie or even a stage show. My grandmother was quite ill at the time and dying. My parents, preoccupied with her, never knew of my truancy.

I spent just enough days in school to qualify to pass, though not enough to really learn anything. Eventually, my years of playing hooky caught up with me.

My first job, at age thirteen, was delivering milk and eggs at five-thirty in the morning for the corner grocer. I did my route in the icy-cold winter mornings before the sun was up. My teeth chattered and my hands were frostbitten from the freezing winds. Because I earned only twenty cents a day, I didn't want to spend a dollar—a week's salary—to buy a flashlight. In the pitch dark, it took me twice as long to find each address.

I used a three-legged pushcart, leaning it on the stoop of the house when I brought up the milk to the apartments. Invariably the push-cart slid down, toppling and cracking the bottles, sending milk into the gutter and scrambled eggs all over the sidewalk. It was not prof-itable, to say the least.

Later, I trained as a furrier, stretching skins until the palms of my hands became raw. I also trained as a jewelry engraver. The boiling hot brown wax that was supposed to hold rings in place leaked and hardened on my fingers; the sharp engraving tool slipped and cut my hands. Tears rolled down my cheeks.

With my rebellious nature and lack of education, I wasn't a very marketable product. My parents, thinking that I must possess *some* ability, made me take violin lessons. After the first lesson, my dis-heartened teacher told my father, "Don't waste your money."

All my early experiences provided valuable training. Even my unsuccessful jobs served as a kind of process of elimination. I found out what I hated to do and where my talents didn't lie.

From these experiences, I learned, and will show you, the way— perhaps the most adventurous and unique way—of creating really enormous gains and undreamed-of wealth.

The waters are rough, but those who swim hard and strong can have it all. After reading this book, you will know how I did it. And, more importantly, how you can do it, too.

But before you get started in the market, ask yourself if you really want to be rich. In truth, some people lack the aspiration or the stomach to become millionaires, nor do they have the backbone for taking risks. They live with those limitations. In this book, I advise people who can handle the risk, who aspire to maximum achievement and maximum wealth.

I promise you, this is the beginning of an exciting new life. Pursue the challenge with enthusiasm. The pursuit of the prize and of great achievement warrants peak excitement. Envision what you want, see yourself achieving the desired goal, and it will come true. See yourself in the condition of success, then work toward it. Don't lie back and wait for it to happen. Keep that vision in your mind daily, constantly work toward it, and you'll be what you dream.

All you need to get rich is this book, the shirt on your back, and a starched, white linen handkerchief in your pocket. Of course, it helps if inside the handkerchief is $400,000 in cash and a quarter of a million dollars in negotiable bonds.

Alternatively, you can amass your personal fortune through astute stock market selection and the specific disciplines that I outline in the following pages. These are the steps that worked for me.

With these strategies, you can create dramatically superior results. You may even do better than I have!

Some days may be less profitable than others, of course. Like children who must touch the hot stove before they understand pain, we all learn through personal experiences and mistakes. I sometimes—in fact, far too often—make mistakes and I'm sure you will, too.

But don't give up. Stay with it. If you do—and if you adhere to the disciplines outlined here—you can do far better than most other people, increasing your chances of success at an extremely competitive game that delivers enormous rewards for superior performance.

Stick to this discipline. Play to perfection and you can win big.

Successful people don't let any grass grow under their feet. As they think about what they want to do—at that instant—they begin.

They value time and know that the way to succeed in the competition that is life—business life, financial life, entrepreneurial life—is to realize that time is the one thing that you must use better than others do.

It's rationed. It's finite. You will never get this minute back again.

Money, wealth, products—these, one may create almost without limitations. But time is so precious it cannot be expanded.

How efficiently you use it, how much positive progress you can achieve in each hour, in each day, will determine whether you will be more successful than the next person, whether you will make your life's work worthwhile.

If you really possess the desire to excel and are willing to persevere and go for it, then start your plan of action.

So who am I and why should what I say carry any weight in your investment decisions?

For the last four decades, I have been a Wall Street investment banker, entrepreneur, economist, investment analyst, and venture capitalist. I am currently Chairman of the Board and sole owner of D.H. Blair Investment Banking Corp., which was established in 1992. Prior to the establishment of D.H. Blair Investment Banking Corp., I was President of D.H. Blair & Co., Inc., which still exists today as a separate and distinct entity from D.H. Blair Investment Banking Corp. Over my career, I have directly or indirectly financed hundreds of companies that have been responsible for the creation of thousands of jobs and billions of dollars in shareholders' equity.

I am proud of the financial track record presented in this book of both D.H. Blair Investment Banking Corp. and D.H. Blair & Co., Inc., while under my leadership. I have endeavored to present in the pages that follow investment insights that I have gained from my separate experiences at the two firms. For ease of reference in this book, I often use terms such as "D.H. Blair," "Blair," "we," and "our" as shorthand for either D.H. Blair Investment Banking Corp. or D.H. Blair & Co., Inc., but readers should keep in mind that, as the context would require, this shorthand refers to two separate entities operating over two separate time periods. Understanding this important distinction will help readers fully appreciate the transactions and advice presented in the pages that follow.

In both 1995 and 1996, *Investment Dealer's Digest, Inc.*, ranked D.H. Blair first in aftermarket performance among underwriters who completed five or more initial public offerings (IPOs) in those years. This means that if, in 1995 or 1996, someone bought a portfolio of IPOs from each underwriter on Wall Street who completed at least five IPOs, the buyer's D.H. Blair IPO portfolio appreciated the most by year-end. And among the underwriters in 1994 who issued seven or more IPOs, Blair again achieved a number one ranking. We were number one in the IPO aftermarket rankings in many other years as well, including 1991, 1987, 1986, 1985, and 1984. Moreover, included in four of these number one portfolios would have been the year's top-performing stock on any exchange in the country. The odds of that happening by chance are extremely low, since thousands of companies are traded on the New York Stock Exchange, the American Stock Exchange, and over the counter.

The cumulative track record of all our companies is pretty extraordinary, considering that it also includes the worst performers and includes all of Wall Street's bad years. Anyone who invested in the over-the-counter market in the mid- to late 1980s knows these were difficult, if not disastrous, periods.

Our IPOs consistently outperformed the indices. In 1996, a basket of the eight Blair new issues rose an average 65.4 percent as measured from offering date to year-end, while comparable baskets invested in the Dow Jones Industrial Index and the NASDAQ Composite Index increased only 16.5 percent and 14.2 percent, respectively.

Blair IPO portfolios, in each of the years from 1980 to 1996, rose on average 44.1 percent from IPO date to year-end, compared to increases of 5.0 percent and 4.6 percent in comparable dollar port-folios in the Dow Jones Industrials and NASDAQ, respectively.

This track record reflects more than luck. It's a matter of total dedication to discovering exciting, emerging small companies and special situations, and maintaining and improving a performance model based on diligence, wisdom, judgment, and faith.

Whatever you've heard about get-rich-quick schemes—and this book does not purport to be one of them—you *can* become rich in the market. That's not fantasy. Success starts with the belief that you can succeed.

No one ever achieved extraordinary success without willing it first. Every great invention, every technological breakthrough, every new business started with an idea. People become millionaires be-cause they challenge reality and follow what those around them said were impossible dreams.

What it takes first of all is vision, then passion, patience, dedica-tion, and endurance. With those ingredients and this book, you can make it happen for you in the stock market and in your life.

This is a book about great dreams and making them come true for you. It is about grand visions and their amazing, impelling power to drive you to enhance your life and to make yourself rich.

This book is about companies that grow from nothing and change the way we work, live, and even think. Companies such as Genetic Systems, which went from an initial unit value of $6 to more than $200 and was bought out for almost $300 million by Bristol-Myers. Companies such as Telepictures, which went from $1,000 to $18,000 per unit and was acquired by Lorimar and, in turn, by Time Warner, one of the biggest media companies in the world. Companies such as Home Centers of America, which increased hundreds of percent in value in one year and was acquired by Kmart, which grew it into a multibillion-dollar company.

Companies in which investments of thousands of dollars would be worth millions today. Companies such as TIE/Communications, which went from a $6 share value to a high of $269, adjusted for splits, and in which a $50,000 investment reached a value of more than $2 million.

New versions of these opportunities are available to you now. But a word of caution: Investing in these types of companies is risky. Nobody knows whether early-stage IPO companies will survive. Finding a level of comfort with such operations is difficult until they really reach a cruising altitude. So it's appropriate—and smart—to exercise caution, even to the point of being skeptical. But remember that the rewards are commensurate with the risks. The highest financial rewards are very often found in venture capital investing.

I speak from the vantage point of four decades of experience. I live and breathe the stock market. I spend almost one hundred hours a week studying, analyzing, and immersing myself in the lifeblood of the market. I've made mistakes along the way, but I believe I've learned as much from my mistakes and losses as from my successes. It took years of intense observation and involvement before I developed an intuitive feel for the market. Knowing which stocks to buy and sell and when to make these transactions. Learning how to act swiftly and decisively in a competitive and turbulent arena. Sensing the changing moods and psychology of the market. Feeling when the investing public and the financial institutions are bullish or bearish—or merely neutral and indifferent.

I gave my life to the acquisition of these skills and this expertise, and in this book I share them with you.

In order to venture into a dynamic, ever-venturesome market, you need a positive temperament. In addition to strength and endurance, you need a happy and positive outlook. Being an optimist is always better than being a pessimist, because an optimist is unhappy only when things are really bad, whereas pessimists are unhappy all the time. Pessimists expect the worst and therefore suffer—both when it's bad and when it's good. So the optimist always does better in this world—and feels better, too—than the pessimist.

Pessimists never see the bright side, the opportunities. Early in my career, for example, I became excited about a number of real estate opportunities. Before the Verrazano Narrows Bridge linked Brooklyn to Staten Island, land now costing $20,000 to $100,000 an acre sold for as little as $75 to $100 an acre. I was eager to invest in this property, which I felt would become very valuable. But a real estate expert I consulted, who never himself bought real estate, didn't share my positive view. He brought in other experts and friends who said the obvious: "What's there? Who knows if the bridge will actually ever get built? If it were worth as much as they're asking and more, why would the present owners be selling it?"

These were respected, outstanding analysts, but they only looked at what was there. They belittled my analysis. They insisted I was a naïve amateur. I said to myself, "Who am I to question these knowledgeable 'experts'?" So they talked me out of a big, winning investment. But making money means you must see what could be—not what is! You must identify the opportunity. You must see it before it's there, before everybody else sees it and wants it. Indeed, you must stick your neck out. It's called "risk." You must act in the face of skepticism and ridicule. It takes guts.

Everyone is a fabulous forecaster after the fact. Winning demands risks.

The reason I do this kind of work is really not for the money. I work in venture capital for the excitement and dynamism of interacting with young entrepreneurs and new companies—forming them, supporting them, seeing their brilliance, imagination, and how worthwhile their new products and technology will be. This delights me profoundly.

I do it because the quality of our lives and certainly those of our children and grandchildren can be positively affected by these entrepreneurs and the companies they launch. These young entrepreneurs, the men and women who generate new jobs, scientific knowledge, and advanced technology, are the real future of America.

Thankfully, many of the transactions I have been involved with have achieved much more than success. They've made an impact on the world.

My wife once wrote up my life story for a journalism course she was taking. Her professor handed it back to her. "Too unrealistic," he scoffed. "These things don't happen in real life." Well, they happened to me!

Ever wondered what quality drives some men and women to achieve the peak of success in their field?

Well, I know, because I—a virtual high school dropout—made millions in the stock market, starting from absolutely nothing! Keep reading and I will show you how I made a fortune through smart investing, and how you can too.

End of Introduction

FROM HARD KNOCKS
TO HOT STOCKS

I

BIG GROWTH
IN SMALL COMPANIES

THE SECRET OF MY SUCCESS

Everyone asks the secret of my success.

I tell them the story of the magician who was working on a cruise ship. He had a parrot that was always ruining his act, saying in the middle of his trick, "The card is up his sleeve," or "He has a rabbit under his hat," or "He slipped it through a hole in his pocket." One day the cruise ship sank. The parrot and the magician found themselves together on a life raft.

For several days, the parrot sat silent and stared at the magician. On the fourth day, the parrot said, "Okay, I give up. What did you do with the ship?"

I willingly share my secret with you.

I set certain goals and then, as I meet those goals, I raise them. That's one of the secrets of life: As you achieve a goal, don't sit back and become satisfied; keep raising your sights and your aspirations. That's what athletes who win Olympic medals do. They achieve results that often seem beyond human attainment and that's what I do, too.

It is like the story of Harry, who one day turned to G-d and said, "Please, G-d, let me win the lottery, I'll give 20 percent of my winnings to charity."

But nothing happened, so a week later Harry turned to G-d again and said, "Please, G-d, let me win the lottery, I'll give 50 percent of my winnings." Still nothing happened. So the next week Harry again appealed to G-d and said, "Please, G-d, let me win the lottery, I'll give 80 percent of my winnings to charity."

Suddenly, in a roaring voice emanating from Heaven, G-d called out to Harry and said, "Harry, give me a break—buy a lottery ticket!"

I put my effort into becoming something. Just wanting or praying for success is not enough.

The harder I work, the "luckier" I get, because not everything I do is right. There were instances in which I lost substantial sums of money, including some in which I lost all—100 percent—of my invested funds. But since I work very hard, I make the unlucky days into better days and turn some lemons into lemonade with my own sweat. By sheer tenacity and persistence, I often accomplish my goals.

A FORMULA FOR SUCCESS AND HAPPINESS

Many of you, particularly those with singular dedication and drive, will achieve outstanding success by following the tenets of this book. And to those of you who do achieve the success, I must add a word of caution. Retain your humility. Just when you think you are a genius, the market will humble you. If you become arrogant, it surely will.

I wear a watch chain. On one end of the chain is my Phi Beta Kappa key, a proud memento of a past achievement. At the other end is a pendant, a present from my wife, on which are engraved the words "This too shall pass." It is a reminder that everything is tenuous. While there is nothing wrong with enjoying our successes, we should be neither too proud nor too depressed, for both the good times and the bad are temporary states and each will pass. This expression is both uplifting and humbling.

You will learn, reading this book, that I've had my head kicked in many times. Perhaps it's inevitable. It's part of life. But each time it happens, I go back to the drawing board and see what I've done wrong and what I've done right in my years on the Street and try to get better at this tough game.

I've seen guys make fortunes and then get so cocky, so convinced of their greatness, their infallibility, their absolute brilliance, that they bring about their own downfall. The Greeks used to caution that those that the gods would destroy, they make godlike first. So always retain your humility. It is necessary for success and for a happy life in this world.

Keep in mind as I do, the old saying, "Who is truly rich? He who is happy with his lot." As you achieve success and your deserved recognition for that achievement, don't get carried away. Wealth is only one dimension of being a success. The most important things in life are not "things."

WAY TO GO!

I carefully think out and determine my objectives.

I don't want to be like the mountaineer who said to his fellow climber, "It almost cost us our lives climbing to the top of Mount Everest to plant the American flag. But it was worth every risk. Hand me the flag."

"Me?" answered his fellow climber. "I thought you brought it!"

I didn't want to be just another successful broker. I wanted to reach the top and leave my mark. I couldn't see myself on the phone selling stocks one at a time for the rest of my life. So once I controlled the firm, I changed my career. I broadened it and made it an adventure instead of a job by taking the firm into new areas.

Before I took over, D.H. Blair was in the money brokerage business. We worked as agents who arranged bank loans for clients, using their stocks and bonds as collateral. This generated much activity but yielded little more than aggravation in return for our efforts.

Over time, I aggressively shifted the focus of the business to venture capital and raising funds for emerging companies.

I remember one partner asking me, "How will we get into it?" He pressured me to hire a consulting firm such as Booz Allen or McKinsey as advisers.

"That's not the way for us," I said. "We'll get into it by doing it." They didn't quite believe me.

I told them one of my favorite stories. Many years ago, New York City wanted to build a tunnel between Brooklyn and Manhattan. They requested bids from contractors. When all the bids were in, the City Council reviewed them. They found that the lowest bid, by far, was made by the Cohen brothers. In fact, the bid was ridiculously low and disproportionate to those of all the other contractors. The Council felt that the Cohen brothers could not possibly meet their estimate, but felt obligated to call them in and speak with them.

"Your bid," said the Council spokesperson, "is by far the lowest and obviously a mistake and we are therefore prepared to let you out of the contract."

The Cohen brothers protested. "We were the low bid so we want the job!"

"But it's impossible," the Council spokesperson asserted. "Tell us how you can do it. How can you possibly be so much lower than any of the other bidders?"

"It's like this," one of the brothers replied. "We don't have the heavy equipment these big firms have. We don't have the overhead. We run a minimum cost operation. I take a shovel and go to the Brooklyn side and start digging. My brother, Max, takes a shovel and goes to the Manhattan side and starts digging. When we meet, you have your tunnel."

"Yes," said the Council spokesperson, "but what happens if you don't meet?"

"Then," replied Sam, "for the same price you get two tunnels!" That's optimism.

I, too, was optimistic: I hoped that I could combine the best aspects of the two Wall Street firms that I admired most and make D.H. Blair a unique and outstanding firm.

REMODELING MODELS

Two firms, C. E. Unterberg, Tobin and Allen & Co., once presented excellent models for emulation in my business.

Unterberg, Tobin was once a leading underwriter for young, emerging companies. It funded many new enterprises and exciting projects. It launched some of the most successful new companies of the 1950s and 1960s, including American Research and Development, Digital Equipment Corp. (DEC), and Ionics. DEC alone rose from a tiny computer company with a valuation of only a few million dollars to a worth of more than $26 billion in the 1980s. Early investors earned thousands of dollars for each $1 invested. It was one of Wall Street's all-time biggest winners. It made many long-term investors immensely rich. I imagined providing equity funding for just such companies and providing my investors with the kind of dramatic wealth enhancement a company like Digital Equipment did.

My second model, Allen & Co., was a small hybrid investment banking company with many innovative people and creative projects going at the same time. All the partners owned pieces of the companies Allen & Co. was involved with, and the partners became rich in the process.

This fit with one of my main goals: recruit people who would join our firm and remain with us because they could work in the securities business and, at the same time, serve as chairmen and presidents of companies we would acquire, or in which we would take substantial equity interests. In the process they would, I hoped, make significant fortunes both for our firm and for themselves. I felt that if I created this type of exciting entrepreneurial organization, where there would be adventure and plenty of money, no one would ever leave D.H. Blair.

My first new hires under this ambitious plan were Jerry Cohen, a member of my synagogue, still attending the Columbia Business School, and Bill Richter, a young graduate of the Harvard Business

School. To be honest, alone each was ineffective. But together and with some help, they became positively dynamic!

One of their first projects was a company called Harvey's Stores.

"We think it's a good buy," they said. "It gives us a chance to own an American Stock Exchange company. Would you help us buy it and get investors involved?"

I backed them and they raised funds from investors. Just starting out, they didn't have much money of their own, but for putting the deal together, they received a fee from D.H. Blair, as well as a small part of the company that they bought.

Thus, while still in their mid-twenties, they became corporate officers. One became board chairman and the other was president of an American Stock Exchange company. It was 1965 and they were each getting $75,000 as officers of the parent holding company they set up. And these were only part-time, titular positions. Of course, they worked diligently, attending board meetings and assisting in the company's financial operations, but it was the subsidiary that required the active hands-on management.

For the two young men, it was the ideal situation and opportunity for doing amazing things. They worked every day at D.H. Blair on mergers, acquisitions, and corporate finance, while building a meaningful annuity and stake in a substantial American Stock Exchange company. For us, it was an ideal situation because we retained two clearly entrepreneurial people and simultaneously participated in exciting deals.

That was precisely my goal—doing what the Unterberg, Tobin and Allen firms did. And we did it, as they did, all out of one office. I admired Allen & Co. because it never expanded its offices, yet at one point it controlled Columbia Pictures. It bought Columbia at $2 a share and sold it to Coca-Cola for many times Allen & Co.'s purchase price. (Coca-Cola later sold it at an even bigger profit!) The people there were imaginative and creative. Their style matched my personality; I, too, like the advantages of being small and exclusive.

Not only did I duplicate what Unterberg, Tobin did in underwriting young companies; inadvertently, I took over their position. Some years ago, they merged with L. F. Rothschild and became a much larger company. Doing larger deals, they left behind the niche they once monopolized and we stepped up in their place.

The Premier Firm

I took D.H. Blair from a money broker and stock sales group to become the premier firm underwriting smaller emerging-growth companies. Since 1980, we have raised nearly $4 billion for these companies of tomorrow. At one time, we had to persuade them to do their initial public offerings through us. Today, they proudly say, "Blair is doing my public offering."

Many of our former competitors for financing IPOs and emerging growth companies—Rooney Pace, Muller, Philips Appel & Walden, Creative Securities, Lomasney, L. M. Rosenthal, and too many others—went out of business.

During this entire period of flourishing and waning enterprises, we were consistently successful for ourselves and most of our clients. We achieved the highest status in our niche of funding emerging growth companies, most of which had no previous track record and carried high risks, as well as potential for exceptional rewards. Our secret in launching these high-risk situations is simple: price them fairly for the public. And we follow, support, and advise these companies throughout their early growth period.

End of chpt. 1

chpt **TWO** *> goes to pg. 25 = 15 pgs.*

NEW IDEAS, NEW ISSUES

The world eagerly awaits new inventions and new ideas. This means investors must identify an early-stage or oncoming vogue, a new pattern of behavior, a revolutionary technology.

Wall Street is like Seventh Avenue. It's important to market what's in vogue. "Emerging growth" is a loosely used term on Wall Street, but we do try to identify true growth fields when underwriting companies: biotechnology; medical technology; computer software; new media communications; neuropharmacology; cellular telecommunications; specialty retail distribution; lasers; environmental control; waste management; and entertainment.

There was a time when almost no one believed biotechnology was even an industry. We first sponsored biotechnology in 1980 with Enzo Biochem, one of the first biotech companies ever taken public. It was a field with enormous potential, indeed one whose impact might equal that of the Industrial Revolution. Today, many of our offerings are still pharmaceutical- or medical-related. Biotechnology is an area that has brought some of our greatest successes.

Less than a decade ago, the feeling on Wall Street about biotechnology was mixed. The bulls thought—as we did—that it could change the way chemicals were made, the way drugs were fashioned, the way waste was destroyed, the way vegetables were grown, and the way animals would breed—that it might even alter human genetic makeup. Its potential was unlimited.

Others were less enthusiastic. Many thought biotech was mostly hype, that the entire concept might quickly dissipate like so much hot air, not nearly as important or immense in scope as its believers foresaw. But even skeptical investors thought it worth watching.

In the movie *The Graduate,* a family friend tells Dustin Hoffman that the secret of the future is plastics. It was a moment of irony, of gently mocking capitalist enthusiasm, but the guy was right. If you invested in plastics when *The Graduate* first appeared, you were part of an enormous growth industry. The institutions and individual investors loved the industry and bought it aggressively. They saw it as a grand-slam home run.

If that movie were made today, the magic word would be biotechnology.

A Grand Slam

Enzo Biochem was a grand slam. It started as a tiny new company with two Iranian brothers and their American brother-in-law making enzymes. They believed that DNA—the molecular substance that contains genetic information—would be a big business and came to us with a proposal for going public as an R&D company.

We initially approached the idea with some trepidation because no one had ever underwritten a company like this before, and we didn't know if we could sell it. Nevertheless, Enzo's management possessed the kind of vision, intellect, and work ethic that makes a great company and we were determined to back them. It was a tough sell. We raised only $4.4 million and the founders gave up 60 percent of the company.

If the public gets half—or more—of a company with the result that 50 cents on every dollar is working on the public's behalf, that is as good a deal for the investor as most any venture capital situation. After all, the founders invested their knowledge, savings, time, and energy—their very lives were spent in product development—bringing their business to a level that was sufficiently convincing and exciting to support a sale to the public.

In this case, we felt that for the founders to give up 60 percent of Enzo Biochem in exchange for $4.4 million was a great deal for the public. Still, selling the shares was hard because the field was completely new, the company unknown, and the future nebulous. There was no other public company like it on the Street.

At that time, most of the people we called on were in the 50 percent or higher tax bracket. "Put up $100,000 or $200,000," I suggested. "We'll take the company public at $6. If you lose, you won't get wiped out. We know the management. They're very cautious, careful people. They don't spend money, they will keep the cash. Worst case, the stock will fall to $3 and you'll lose half your money. Your $100,000 investment will still be worth $50,000 and, after taxes, your loss will be $25,000 if you're in the 50 percent bracket." If they were in a slightly higher bracket, 55 or 60 percent, the loss would have been less.

"On the other hand, if it works," I said, "it could be a $50 stock or more. So you're talking about making nine or ten times your money on a $100,000 investment. You could make maybe a million dollars!"

Wealthy investors are receptive to that kind of risk. They already know how to make 10 to 15 percent on their money, so they're open to unusual recommendations. They like a situation that might, if successful, significantly impact their wealth. It appeals to them on a capital gains basis.

That's why we were effective in selling Enzo.

Enzo ultimately went from $6.25 not merely to $50, but it rose to the equivalent of nearly $200 per share adjusted for stock splits. This progress certainly took time and grudging industry acceptance of the exciting product Enzo developed. It brought out a DNA probe that is nonisotopic. When released, this probe represented a dramatic scientific breakthrough.

Enzo eventually clocked in with almost three hundred different patents, some of which have given it dominant positions in the marketplace.

Investors, friends, and clients of mine bought homes based on their Enzo investment. One of them refers to his exquisite residence as "the house that Enzo built," because he bought the stock early and added to it constantly. By pyramiding, which I will discuss later, he made a great deal of money.

In 1982, Johnson & Johnson invested $14 million in company stock at a substantial premium above market price and then many more millions in research funds, helping Enzo develop the DNA probe for a portion of Johnson & Johnson's product line.

How did Enzo achieve such spectacular popularity and tremendous appreciation in the price of its stock? The people who believed Enzo was revolutionary bought aggressively and kept buying. Those who felt it might be as big as the chemical industry also bought in. Even those who were skeptics, institutions as well as individuals, bought some stock because they couldn't afford not to be part of it, in case the real industry optimists at the other end, those who believed biotech was a leading edge growth area, turned out to be right.

After a while, everybody went for biotechnology, hedging their embarrassment if it turned explosive and they missed out. Perhaps they bought it less aggressively or only at an earlier stage when it was still at a low price. But they did get involved.

Enzo's success inspired us to do Genetic Systems, which was launched out of our offices. At the time of its founding, it was just a concept—no office space or even any money in the bank. We raised $6 million for them in an initial public offering. But because there were warrants attached to the stock, we ultimately raised about $35 million in total. In 1986, the company was sold to Bristol-Myers for $300 million in stock. Today that Bristol-Myers stock is worth close to $1 billion.

Thus, an early-stage company, valued at perhaps $20 million when we took it public, was sold after five years for what grew into close to $1 billion.

The company began with no meaningful profits at the time, but its product development was phenomenal, and Bristol-Myers saw some products as potential major medical and pharmaceutical break-throughs.

This arena presents the kind of risk-reward situation that everyone who can tolerate the risk-reward equation should be involved with. It provides immense possibilities for a home run.

Following Enzo, we underwrote a number of new biotechnology companies and we raised more money for totally new start-ups than Goldman Sachs or Morgan Stanley. At Blair, we helped launch more genetics companies than anybody on Wall Street because we love their imaginative, dynamic managements and because we like the future prospects for this most promising field.

A WINNER IS CALLING

My philosophy in biotechnology translated well to other potential IPO fields, including telecommunications.

A company that did spectacularly well in telecommunications early on was TIE/Communications. I invested $100,000 in the company not long after AT&T lost its monopoly. Carterfone Communications audaciously challenged AT&T, announcing that it would sell telephones to companies and to individuals. It was unheard of at the time. The case wound up in court.

The *Carterfone* decision permitting the company to sell telephones would transform the telephone industry. Years earlier, after Eastman Kodak lost its monopoly on film developing, a number of companies emerged as major players in a few years. These were very exciting companies providing rich rewards to their founders and investors.

When I looked for an investment in the telephone industry field, I identified TIE, a company that promised growth.

TIE was started by Tom Kelley, a fellow who left AT&T, and his lawyer, Len Fassler. They were a powerful combination. I put up $100,000 early on and ultimately earned $14 million on my investment.

Yet, at one time during the unequal struggle between the giant American Telephone and its tiny new competitors, I almost sold my own $100,000 stake for less than $5,000.

We went through hell and TIE went to the brink of bankruptcy because of AT&T's claim that the entire United States telephone system would be wrecked if the new competitors' phones were connected to its system. AT&T insisted TIE customers buy and install an interface between the existing system and these new phones at $100 per phone connection.

That hurt TIE badly. Major companies like Litton went into the phone marketing and installation business, but when their customers learned they had to pay a $100 charge to purchase the required interface, they wouldn't buy the phones and the buyers sent them all back to us. We had $7 million in debt owed to Chemical Bank and less than $1 million in stockholder equity. On a cash basis we were literally bankrupt.

Chemical could have put us back on the brink of bankruptcy, because our only collateral was warehouses full of phones. But I think they hypothesized that even if they put nothing but phones on everyone's desk in all of their branch banks, they would still have too many phones. They turned us over to their factoring division, Domerick, and we paid 4 percent over prime during the 1970s, when the prime went over 15 percent. Paying 16 percent or more for our loans meant we were literally working for the bank for the rest of the decade.

For several years, the bank made more money than we did; in fact, we made no money while they made lots.

Fortunately for us, the Supreme Court ultimately ruled against the telephone company and stripped away the interface requirement, holding that it was merely a guise to block competition. The result was the explosive growth that we always anticipated. That's when my patient $100,000 turned into a value of $14 million.

This demonstrates another case of identifying an industry and a company which might make it big and living through the inevitable, harrowing, stomach-churning events that eventually, with faith and patience, can really pay off.

Though we fought for almost ten years, in the end it was tremendously rewarding and gratifying for me, but more importantly, for our clients. In terms of its stock price appreciation, TIE became one of the most successful underwritings in the history of D.H. Blair.

Everyone was skeptical about another of our companies, Telepictures, because it started out purchasing a small film library out of bankruptcy from Chemical Bank. The company produced impressive revenues and earnings from this acquired library, but it was felt that this was a one-time, nonrecurring, nonduplicable situation. What would they do for an encore after they syndicated their films to South American and European countries so hungry for this relatively blah product? But Telepictures became a major company and merged with Lorimar, which in turn subsequently merged into Time Warner. Again, it was based on betting on the jockeys, Mike Solomon and Mike Garin. They became officers and major stockholders in Lorimar-Telepictures. Although the merger was an achievement, Telepictures, even on its own, ran lucky, producing such enormously profitable TV shows as *The People's Court* and acquiring such winners as the *I Love Lucy* series. It became a major company in television syndication and production.

HOME TO MILLIONS

In the case of Home Centers of America, Frank Denny and a group of jockeys came to us with an already impressive track record. They ran a company called Handy Dan for W. R. Grace and built a successful wholesale warehouse concept. They wanted to launch a new company on their own and needed start-up money.

We liked what we saw and raised $6 million for half the company. The units went from $6 to $55 during the course of their first year. Then investors exercised warrants, and the company raised an additional $8 million in a secondary offering. Just thirteen months after we raised the $6 million, Home Centers of America was sold to Kmart for $94 million—from a zero start.

At that time it was breaking even, only beginning to make money, and we got close to $100 million for it. Under Kmart, it grew to maybe $3 billion a year in sales. Perhaps we sold too quickly! In hindsight, Home Depot, a major competitor and leader in the same field, grew at a phenomenal compounded growth rate of approximately 100 percent a year for nearly a decade. It proved one of the most rewarding stock market investments of the last decade. Or maybe Home Centers needed Kmart's support and additional capital. In any case, it turned into a big winner for them and very rewarding for us and our risk-taking investors.

Home Centers was a start-up. Hardly the first of its kind, but it represented a new concept that was coming increasingly into vogue—category killer warehouses, holding everything for the home improvement market. These warehouses proliferated in the West and Southwest and Home Centers rode that trend.

CELLULAR SELLS

Another telecommunications sleeper we helped launch that turned into a major score was American Cellular Network (AmCell). Its entrepreneurial founders bid for the airwaves over which car phones and other wireless phones would communicate.

It was a complete start-up, just an idea, but the principals were powerful guys: Sidney Azeez, the Chairman, was a successful venture capitalist and John Scarpa was well known in communications. The cellular airwave industry, Azeez told us, was explosive—like FM radio in its first days—but much faster and potentially more lucrative than just selling cellular phones because they were buying monopolies.

In addition, other successful business people bought into the company because they believed in these entrepreneurial principals.

We raised $4.5 million for half the company.

The shares opened at a premium at the height of the IPO market in 1983 and then, in just a few weeks, fell apart as the market collapsed. For several years the stock drifted around the offering price as the field remained full of uncertainty. First the smaller players, who the Federal Communications Commission (FCC) thought might not see a project through, were eliminated. AmCell was a small company, but with good financing and strong players.

Then the FCC decided that the awards would be made by lottery, making the whole enterprise a real crapshoot.

AmCell's principals prepared a large number of good proposals at relatively little cost and made multiple bids, which—just like a lottery—increased their chances of winning. A number of bidders formed a consortium. By winning a few areas and negotiating shrewdly, AmCell ended up with franchises in Las Vegas (which it won by lottery) and some important areas along the East Coast—but really no major ones. The most noteworthy was Reading, Pennsylvania, hardly a major metropolis. Nevertheless, it turned out to be a home run, in fact, a grand-slam home run.

The company was valued at $8 million in mid-1983 when we first brought it out and didn't show much price action for several years, but in early 1988, a mere five years after we first brought it public as a total start-up, it was bought out by Comcast for $230 million.

PATLEX PATENTLY SUPERIOR

Some of our successes have been more than financial victories; they were moral victories, such as when we helped the true inventor of the laser, Dr. Gordon Gould. The laser was one of the most significant technological innovations of our generation. Unfortunately, for more than thirty years, Dr. Gould struggled in court to prove that he was indeed the rightful inventor. When no one else showed an interest in financing his continued battle, our due diligence gave us the conviction that his was a good case.

We did a $4.8 million financing for his company, Patlex Corporation, because we believed in his breakthrough and in his case. In this instance, the results for his company were spectacular.

On November 4, 1987, the U.S. Patent Office awarded Dr. Gould the patent for the Gas Discharge Laser. As a result, Patlex was probably the only stock that doubled in the month following the October stock market crash of 1987.

The beautiful irony of this award is that this patent now runs for seventeen years and, of course, the laser is ubiquitous today—in most retail outlets, automation systems, and many medical devices. Ironically, if Dr. Gould had won the patent in 1957, its seventeen years would have run out before the value and significance of his breakthrough translated into major products.

Today, Patlex collects royalties from GTE, AT&T, Ford, Motorola, Honeywell, and other major companies. *Forbes* magazine estimates that Dr. Gould's laser patents cover 90 percent of the lasers used in the United States and are worth between $100 and $200 million.

DR. SALK'S LEGACY GROWS

In recent years, we targeted and recruited leading thinkers and scientists in specific disciplines where their genius could be directed toward the needs of society.

The quest for an effective AIDS vaccine is an area of national concern where we often focus our funding efforts. One example is The Immune Response Corporation. We initiated the formation of this company with the renowned inventor of the polio vaccine, Dr. Jonas Salk, to help develop his unique postexposure AIDS vaccine. We invested our own seed capital and then raised several million dollars at $1 a share in a private placement.

Subsequently, major corporate investors such as Rorer Group, Colgate-Palmolive, and State Farm Insurance invested $30 million before the company was brought public at $7 a share by Dillon, Read & Co. It attained a high of $60 a share in late 1991 before selling off in the disillusionment with biotech that set in for a while when market enthusiasm for this group temporarily got overcooked.

A Harvard classmate of mine, who was the principal of one of Wall Street's most elite boutiques, invested $100,000 for 100,000 shares and in two and a half years cashed in $4 million. And he didn't even sell out at the top!

But, perhaps most importantly, if Immune Response's science led by Dr. Salk could anywhere near approach his achievement in obliterating the dreaded polio disease, it would be more gratifying than any material achievement I could ever attain, no matter how lucrative. That would be the greatest reward for which I would ever wish.

BREAKTHROUGH SCIENCE PRODUCES BREAKTHROUGH PRODUCTS

Initially formed in October 1988, Interneuron Pharmaceuticals, Inc., is a prime example of combining breakthrough science with top-notch management to build a company from scratch. To help form the company around advanced research being done at the Massachusetts Institute of Technology, and to fund the company's operations during its first year, Blair and its clients privately invested a total of approximately $2.4 million in Interneuron. In March 1990, we underwrote Interneuron's initial public offering and raised $9.3 million.

In the years since its formation, Interneuron has become a premier pharmaceuticals company with a robust product pipeline. The company's products address large markets and serious medical areas, including stroke, heart disease, obesity, Parkinson's Disease, and sleep disorders. Interneuron has also formed several subsidiaries and established joint ventures with major global pharmaceutical firms. Its product pipeline contains numerous compounds spanning the preclinical to postclinical phases.

Since its early-stage funding provided by Blair, Interneuron has raised many tens of millions of additional capital through major Wall Street firms, international business partners, and warrant exercise. Like Amgen, Genentech, and Chiron, three biotech superstars that provided investors with sensational returns, Interneuron has the breakthrough science and products to be one of the outstanding technology growth companies of the next decade.

A PREMIER COMPANY

An even more recent example of an exciting company that we were able to identify early on as potentially a big winner, but that seemed to elude many of our competitors, is Premier Laser Systems. Premier was formed in 1991 through a management buyout of Pfizer Laser Systems, a division of Pfizer Hospital Products Group, Inc. By 1994, Premier had an accumulated deficit of approximately $9 million, primarily incurred through the company's research efforts to develop its surgical, optical, and dental laser systems.

Although the company had been cleared by the FDA to market several types of general surgical lasers, it was losing money and needed additional capital to continue R&D and pursue clinical trials on a variety of innovative products. In particular, Premier had developed a "hard-tissue" dental laser which could be used to "drill" tooth cavities painlessly, but the company needed money to complete clinical trials before the device could be cleared to market by the FDA.

So with under $2 million in annual sales and years of multimillion dollar losses as a financial track record, Premier sought additional capital. After being turned down by several venture capitalists and investment banks, including one underwriter who started but then backed out of a financing deal, Premier came to Blair. In the spring of 1994, we agreed to underwrite the company's initial public offering and also to provide $1.6 million in an interim bridge loan.

But then, during that summer, Premier became involved in litigation with its sole supplier of a specialized optic fiber required for use in one of Premier's lasers. This supplier ceased to provide the required fiber to Premier in favor of one of the company's competitors. While the onset of litigation of any kind can often adversely affect a company's ability to complete an IPO, we decided to proceed with the financing after due diligence on all the issues surrounding the litigation and the impact it potentially could have on the company. We successfully completed a $13.8 million IPO for Premier in November 1994.

In the two years following the initial public financing, Premier continued to develop and test its lasers in the clinic. Unfortunately, as is often the case with medical research, the clinical trials extended beyond their initial schedules, and the delay resulted in Premier's again needing additional financing. To raise the capital necessary to continue, Premier negotiated with a well-known underwriter to complete a public secondary stock offering. As if history were repeating itself, that underwriter was unable to complete the offering. So we stepped in once again. Through Blair, Premier raised $12.7 million in October of 1996. Now the company was poised to make history.

In May 1997, Premier announced that its hard-tissue laser had been the first of its kind cleared to market by the FDA. Since laser drills don't vibrate or require local anesthesia, the company's stock price jumped as investors scrambled to get in on the next generation of dental equipment. Indeed, Premier's hard-tissue laser represented a breakthrough in dentistry. Thanks in large part to the efforts of this start-up company, dental patients will in the very near future no longer have to suffer the anxiety of conventional drilling.

OPPORTUNITIES FAR AND AWAY

In the same way that we recognize the high growth potential of biotech and medical companies, we also appreciate the lucrative opportunities that exist overseas. U.S.-China Industrial Exchange, Inc. (Chindex), and First South Africa Corp. are two such companies that we brought public.

In August 1994, we raised $9.2 million in an initial public offering for Chindex, an independent marketing and sales organization that operates in the People's Republic of China. The company provides manufacturers from the U.S., Europe, and various countries with access to the Chinese marketplace. It mainly focuses on the marketing and selling of products with a medical or industrial orientation.

First South Africa Corp., another international company that we took public, acquires, owns, and operates seasoned, closely held industrial and consumer product companies in South Africa with sales in the $5 million to $50 million range. In January 1996, we raised $11.5 million for First South Africa Corp. It is the first publicly traded company in the United States making direct investments in South African–operated companies.

Over the years, we were fortunate and cautious enough to choose companies and industries in which big money is likely to be made.

In the last analysis, however, the most gratifying aspect of this work is the knowledge that we have been engaged in true capitalism—creating real wealth in terms of these new products and technologies.

When we fund companies, we generate new jobs—literally as soon as the very next day. It is these small emerging companies that, *chpt. 2 (cont)*

25.

upon their initial formation and by their continued expansion, create new jobs.

Every new product or service, every remarkable invention, every medical breakthrough, every new job established, makes America and the world a healthier and happier place in which to live.

End of chpt. 2

Chpt. 3) goes to pg. 36 = 10 pgs

THREE

ADVENTURES IN VENTURE LAND

When I was a kid, we still had iceboxes that were stocked daily with large blocks of ice. Radio had just come into its own. Our radios had huge vacuum tubes in them. They were as large as refrigerators and designed like little cathedrals.

But in 1959, when I started in the investment business, the prevailing feeling among research analysts was that the age of great inventions and opportunities was over.

People felt the world would no longer see industries and companies arise from nothing to assume dominant positions in the marketplace. RCA developed in the 1920s; General Electric and General Motors were mature. The prevailing attitude was that there was no room for more enterprise on this grand scale.

Only a few years after World War II, I heard people repeatedly say the big opportunities had passed them by—it was too late for them. And even as early as the 1900s, European immigrants who arrived in the United States were told by their predecessors, "Now you come. It's all over. You missed it all—it's too late, the fortunes have been made." It seems it's always too late.

Yet, in the decades since I started, countless numbers of new companies have started up from nowhere and grown bigger than their dreams. MCI, Intel, Compaq, Syntex, Xerox, Microsoft, Genentech, and Home Depot became stars. In fact, Microsoft, founded in 1975, has made Bill Gates worth more than $40 billion and the richest man in America.

When I was at the Harvard Business School from 1957 to 1959, we used slide rules for math computations. The calculators we take for granted today had not yet been invented. Even at Loeb Rhoades, which seemed to be in the vanguard of change when I worked there in the summer of 1958, primitive calculators were just beginning to come into use, and they were giant-sized. Now we all have tiny calculators that do much more than the original devices and can be carried in a vest or coat pocket.

Computers were once mammoth instruments. You used to need the space of several rooms to hold one of them. Now you have desktop and laptop miniature computers that hold more information than those old dinosaurs. Amazingly, computers once priced at a few million dollars now cost a few thousand and provide far more capacity.

The semiconductor had not yet been invented. When chips were first manufactured, perhaps less than 2 percent of them out of a lot were viable. The remaining 98 percent were thrown away. Today they've gone through a spectacular evolution. They've become infinitely better in quality and you can put more information on a chip smaller than your fingernail than you could on ten thousand when they were first invented.

For the first eighteen hundred years of recorded history, there was practically no change in the speed which people traveled. The maximum achievable speed was about what a horse does at a gallop—20 or 30 miles an hour at most. And now, every ten years, we see an exponential compounding of that rate. Some missiles go 1,000 or more meters per second, and military aircraft can exceed the speed of sound.

The term biotech, which captures possibly the most exciting of all recent technologies, wasn't even coined yet.

New Companies, New Hope

This rapid rate of change was accompanied by an equally rapid growth of opportunity for, and interest in, new companies. Developing early-stage companies weren't seen as the future; in fact, the reverse was true. The mature companies were everybody's favorite. General Motors owned the auto market, competing with long-lost household brands such as Packard, Hudson, Studebaker, and DeSoto.

Isn't that ironic? They were great companies—you can remember the names. But now they're historical trivia. In the meantime, auto companies that didn't exist fifty years ago now hold center stage.

Many of these companies were born in the last twenty-five years and they were great, great buys. In the early seventies, a friend of mine suggested that I invest in Subaru. I didn't. Had I put $100,000 into that idea, by the late seventies it would have been worth many millions.

Emergent opportunities provide the biggest plays, the best chance for you to become immensely wealthy. They may be new companies or they may be new industries. They require their own investment strategies.

Based on my personal experience, I still feel the biggest fortunes are to be made by the individual investor identifying and investing in emerging or young companies.

They may not be listed on a major exchange. They generally are not. They are most likely to be listed and quoted on the NASDAQ stock market. Their sales may be almost zero because they are just starting to develop. Yet they may be the next Intel or Microsoft, the new Polaroid or Syntex.

I remember when the market for Syntex was born on the theme or the expectation that there would be a pill to control birth. A birth control pill. What a novel idea it was then!

Everyone was skeptical and it was hard to buy Syntex in terms of standard criteria. The company had no meaningful sales or earnings. Everyone asked: Is it real? Will it work? What about the side effects?

Will it get FDA approval? The professional traders shorted the stock, confident they could buy it back much cheaper, expecting that the pill was phony and would never come to fruition. Or they thought that if it came to fruition, no one would buy it or that even if they did buy it, the side effects would be dangerous. Even if the side effects weren't dangerous, it was just one product, they thought. What would the company do next? Won't other companies come along and compete?

Every developing new company attracts skeptics and shorters— traders that sell it short and publicly bash it—because in the early stages the company trades on still uncertain future expectations—on hope and dreams.

Be a Believer—and Never Sell Short

That is why the opportunities are there: because only a very few believe the story. You will find the greatest opportunities in these new companies, but you will also find the greatest skepticism and the most shorts. As the stock goes up in price, more and more people say, "It's overpriced, it has nothing, it has no reason to be there." And so they sell it with the intention of buying it back cheaper. This is a dangerous game, because in due course, they will buy it back to cover their short, sometimes at a much higher price.

This is the way shorting works. If you go short 1,000 shares at $10, you are selling shares you do not own for $10,000. You will have to buy them back because you borrowed the stock that you're selling and must return it. If the stock goes to $5, you can buy it back for $5,000 and make a $5,000 profit. But if it goes to $20, you'll have to pay $20,000 and lose $10,000. If the stock goes to $100, you can lose $90,000 and if it goes to $200, you can lose $190,000, even though you only put up $10,000 originally.

This is the big difference in risk between being long and being short. When you are long, when you purchase the shares, the most you can lose is 100 percent—in this case your absolute maximum risk of loss would have been the $10,000 you invested. But when you are short, there is no limit to the loss on the upside. My advice, therefore, is simple: Never sell short! You should always keep the risk-reward ratio in your favor.

I learned this lesson the hard way many years ago when I went short on, of all companies, Microsoft. My reasoning seemed sensible enough at the time. At over sixty times earnings, Microsoft's price/earnings ratio (P/E) appeared outrageously high. Instead of following my own proven advice, which I will discuss later, of buying at the new high—which would have made me hundreds of percent over time—I bet the stock would fall. In brief, I got killed on this one, losing hundreds of percent as Microsoft kept producing higher earnings and an even higher stock price.

So never sell short; it's a negative bet with a limited payoff. Even if you are right on your bet that a stock price will fall, the absolute most you can make is 100 percent of the value of the stock if the price falls to zero. This, of course, is unlikely, and is not even what you are expecting when you sell a stock short. You're probably expecting to make 20 percent to 30 percent if your negative bet is correct. Accordingly, I recommend that you focus on picking winners, rather than losers. Your upside on winners is potentially hundreds of percent, and your downside is only the amount of your investment.

THE SIZZLE SELLS BETTER THAN THE STEAK

If you want to make a true fortune, pick an early-stage company that will eventually make it. That's what I spend my time trying to do. Over the past two decades, many issues we underwrote at $5 or $6 traded at over $100 within a few short years. As a rule, you just don't find that magnitude of price appreciation on the Big Board.

Those inflated prices are not always justified. Inevitably, some of the stocks are overpriced and come back down, proving not to be worth anywhere near their highest valuations.

Nevertheless, the point is this: The expectations, the dreams, sell better than the realities. On Wall Street, sizzle sells better than steak. By the time the steak is ready, by the time the company develops a P/E ratio and its present value and growth potential are more identifiable, it just doesn't sell at as high a price. It's no longer an exciting dream.

A mature company can generally move only in relation to the economy as a whole. It *is* the economy, or at least an integral part of it. It cannot grow at some exponential rate unrelated to overall economic growth.

Hopefully, what we want to do is get you, the risk-taking investor, into a "dream" stock early, at a very exciting risk-reward valuation, and let the rest of the world take it away later.

The greatest multiple of earnings, the seemingly infinite ones, occur when the product is still an expectation. Everybody talks about it. It *will* cure cancer or it *will* grow hair on your head. Frankly, its price is not even in touch with reality, because nobody knows what it is worth.

A small company, however, can indeed grow from $1 million to $100 million, even if the economy is declining, if it has some new, increasingly desirable product, such as semiconductors or computers, that suddenly develops a market. Similarly, the unique company, one with something extra going for it, represents a "special situation." A special situation is typically distinguished as a stock that—because of certain characteristics—may rise in price independent of the general market. The most obvious of these characteristics is a takeover possibility.

Until very recently, even IBM was growing each year, through every single recession that we had. A number of companies can do that and grow even faster. These are real growth companies—Coca-Cola, McDonald's, Toys "R" Us. They command very high multiples of their earnings, which is what really matters. That's how you get the big moves and the high prices.

Remember, we go for the big hit. Inevitably, the biggest stock winners attract the most skeptics and the largest short positions.

Occasionally, the shorts do turn out to be right. A stock gets ahead of itself and becomes very overpriced. Or the product never materializes. Or, before it materializes, someone comes up with an even better product. Then it really does turn out to be a bubble, a dream.

But if you have an Intel or a Microsoft or an Élan Corp., which we took public fifteen years ago and whose profits keep growing at a remarkable annual rate, the shorts become a positive. Once the stock starts moving up, the shorts must buy it back, because their losses are potentially unlimited. They're afraid that they'll go bankrupt, and they can. No matter how rich you are, you can lose it all if you sell something that you don't own and it keeps moving up and up. You keep getting margin calls and you have to put up your money until you cover the short by buying it in or until you run out of money to put up.

About ten years ago, the prevailing story goes, one of the smartest short sellers in the history of Wall Street made one of the Street's most disastrous moves by persistently shorting Resorts International. He shorted it at an average price of about $15, ultimately building a short position of 200,000 to 250,000 shares. In just months, Resorts International soared to $60, $120, and then almost $150—impossible numbers—and the stock reportedly was at its high when he covered most of his short. If this story is even partly true, he could have lost $20 million to $30 million.

This famous shorter thought the price was unjustified. He turned out to be wrong. Resorts was the first casino to open in Atlantic City, in what was then brand-new gambling territory, and it turned out to be a phenomenal winner—until it overleveraged and suffered a dramatic reversal. If people had shorted Polaroid's "implausible"

invention—an instant camera—they would certainly have lost a fortune, too.

Sometimes you can become a winner just by believing in the
unbelievable.

Opportunity exists in dream companies and special situations simply because the risks are so eminently obvious, the distance to success
so great, and the potential for failure so imminent, that most investors
are reluctant to buy them. There's a lack of urgency to buy now
because the reality, the goal, seems so remote. The company has little
or no sales or earnings. It seems way ahead of itself by any reasonable
criterion: price, earnings, or definitive proof for the possibility of a
product in many cases.

That's the opportunity!

IMPACT YOUR WEALTH

People worth a few million dollars want to know how to make
more than 10 or 15 percent on their money. "I have $5 million,"
they say. "How can I make it into $10 million?"

If you want to move toward doubling your wealth, which will take
a lot, put $200,000 into a stock such as an emerging biotech company.
Use your own due diligence, see for yourself what promising technology it has, and if you believe in its potential, then make that $200,000
investment. Wait and see how it does half a year down the road. If it
doesn't work, you might lose half your money, $100,000. If it looks
lousy before year-end, sell it. The government will absorb 30 percent
to 40 percent or more of the loss and you'll end up losing only 30 percent to 40 percent of your initial investment. Given the size of your
wealth, it won't have more than a minor impact.

But, on the upside, it could go up anywhere from five times to
twenty-five times and more, and in that case that $200,000 would
be worth $1 million, $2 million, or even $5 million depending on
how successful and how accurate the results are.

Some rich people like that. They say, "Okay, buy me $200,000 worth. Maybe I'll lose sixty or seventy grand, or I'll make $3 or $4 million or only $2 million." It really can impact their wealth, which is what they want, and they don't mind the risk. They can afford the loss if it comes to that, but they love the potential for an enormous payoff. That is why some of them drill wildcat oil wells.

In a way, that is what I am doing. I like the excitement and the risk of wildcat drilling. The bigger risk and bigger reward are perfect for young people who can afford to lose almost everything and go for it again. But this strategy is *not* appropriate for an elderly person who needs all of his or her money to live on. If older people lose it, they're not likely to get another chance at making their money back. But young people should see how far they can expand their muscles before they just settle.

This kind of stock is hard to buy psychologically. It isn't based on "proven reality." You say, "Gee, I'm paying a lot for a company that has no earnings." Maybe not even a product that will ever command a significant market. People are much more comfortable buying something like General Motors, though it's probably going nowhere or has only limited upside potential. Unlike GM, the new company is hard to live with, hard to sleep with. Its price gyrates and it is vulnerable to any bad news—a missed contract, a delay in its product development, a bad quarter, earnings or orders disappointments.

HARD TO SELL A WINNER

The companies destined to be the biggest winners are the ones I've had the hardest time selling—not only to my clients but to my own brokers. In fact, I often miss good opportunities because when I get on the phone to sell the stock, the response can be so negative that this, in turn, influences me. I tell myself, "Maybe they're right. Maybe I am overenthusiastic. Maybe I'm getting all carried away." Yet a year later, the company is often flying high.

Skepticism is precisely why such companies are good values. Sane, rational investors want no part of them. They're out of favor . . . so they're undervalued.

There's something to contrarianism. When the public is in love with a stock and buying it like crazy, my gut instinct says "Sell!" When they don't like it, when they're skeptical and that skepticism is overdone, as it often is, then it is a good buy.

You will often see a stock come way down right after good earnings are reported. On the face of it, it doesn't seem to make sense. If the company reports good earnings, why is the stock down? The reason is that many people felt the success coming; they already knew about the company's good performance and healthy earnings long before the accountant's report was issued. The good news about the company has already been reflected in the stock price. By the time of the earnings report, which is when the less sophisticated people rush to buy, it's a good time to cash in your profits.

Conversely, when a company reports terrible earnings, terrible losses, or a big write-off, stocks may, surprisingly, run up. Here, the market has already discounted, that is, already anticipated, the bad quarter, as reflected in the depressed price of the stock. Once the bad news is confirmed, there's room to be optimistic about the future.

The essence of the market is that it discounts the future on new dream stocks, too. Market prices of stock are all based on the hope that a particular industry is an industry of the future or that a particular company is the company of the future, one that will offer revolutionary, vital, rewarding new products. The pharmaceutical company with a new, exciting product will sell at a far higher price than many of the established drug companies because such a company has the sizzle and the dream. It is where you want to be; it is where you can make your fortune.

End of chpt.3

chpt. 4 } gres to pg: 45 = 9ff0.

FOUR

PROFITS AND PROPHECIES

A monk joined a monastery of the strictest order; he was only allowed to speak three words a year.

At the end of his first long year he came before the head monk and said "food no good." A year later he again came before the head monk and said "bed too hard." At the end of his third frustrating year he once again came before the head monk and said, "I'm going home."

The head monk looked up at him and said, "I'm not surprised. All you've done since you came here is complain."

People often complain about the market. But, in truth, if you review the performance of stocks and alternative liquid investments, you'll find that stocks are terrific at generating gains. From 1926 through 1996, the mean annual return from large company stocks was 12.7 percent, compared with only 6.0 percent for long-term corporate bonds and 3.8 percent for U.S. Treasury bills. And the inflation rate averaged 3.2 percent a year during this period. So Treasury bills—the "safest" investment—adjusting for inflation—gave no real return.

Even more relevant and noteworthy, small-cap companies—those with market values under $100 million—gave long-term investors the very best returns—17.7 percent a year, which compares favorably with returns on large company stocks and on corporate and government bonds.

In a seventy-year study of the rewards from investing in small, emerging growth company stocks as against the rest of the market, Ibbotson Associates showed that $1,000 invested in such companies in 1925 was worth $4.5 million in 1996. This return was more than three times greater than that of large-cap stocks and almost three hundred times that of U.S. Treasury bills for the same period. Emerging growth stocks, the instruments with the greatest risk, gave the greatest returns. Treasury bills, the instruments with the smallest risk, gave the smallest returns. A natural state of affairs, when you think about it.

The only drawback is that stocks, particularly small-cap stocks, gyrate unpredictably over the short term. If you seek the greatest rewards, you must live with the most volatility as well as the most emotional upheaval and psychic aggravation. There is no gain without pain. That is the reality with which you must live.

Over the long term, stocks, particularly small-cap stocks, have been the best performers in the American capitalist system. They are simply the best place to put your money. The risks you run are when you invest needed capital and are thus forced to sell your stocks at an inopportune time. This means you should invest only your speculative capital, the capital you have tucked away for the far future— not your living capital.

UP, UP, AND AWAY

Your choice of a stock makes a big difference in your return on investment. That 12.7 percent growth rate for large company stocks represents a long-term average return. I always look to do better than average. I look for the exceptional person, the one with the faith and the ability to invest in the emerging growth stocks that, intelligently selected, will yield far better returns than 12.7 percent, 22.7 percent, or even 32.7 percent.

If you have the opportunity to buy growth companies, either at the initial public offering or immediately thereafter, and if you pick one of the outstanding winners, you will do brilliantly.

Some stocks come down after attaining their highs—perhaps 30 percent and sometimes more. This is not surprising, since they come down only after going up as much as 1,000 percent. All stocks have tops and I'm not saying that all growth stocks are permanent buys.

Growth stocks are not for everyone. You must have the stomach for them. For example, during the bear market of 1973–1974, stocks lost over a third of their value. In October 1987, just after the market crash, many of us thought we were finished, kaput. When you're going through that kind of down market, it adds precious little to your happiness to know that over a seventy-year period—from 1925 to 1996—the average annual return has been close to 12.7 percent. It does you very little good to know that if you are experiencing a loss of 36 percent on your investment in a single year. Nevertheless, history suggests that over the very long term you will average 12.7 percent, and the largest returns—far better than 12.7 percent—are generated by the small-cap companies.

WORRY YOUR WAY TO WEALTH

An extremely negative article came out in March 1987 in a prominent business publication about Organogenesis, a company that we had brought public a few months earlier and that was involved in developing an artificial skin. The article, entitled "Speculative Heat," was incredibly skeptical and stressed all the risks.

Yet even as it knocked the company, this publication acknowledged that "if Organogenesis's theory works, it will be revolutionary. Only don't start the parade just yet." This is how the financial press typically knocks young stocks—and it is simply part of the risk you must live with in investing in such stocks—not to mention the worry and attacks of nerves as you wait for proven results.

Even with the warnings and the criticism, Organogenesis's stock more than doubled only a few months after the article was written. Such results don't necessarily mean that over the long term Organogenesis will be a big winner. However, the original units we brought out went from $16 to the equivalent of over $125. The warrants were converted, the stock split 2 for 1, and the company now trades on the American Stock Exchange.

These are the exciting opportunities: Funding a small young company that the big guys are knocking. But the company's product is not yet a proven technology. If it were, it wouldn't be selling at these relatively attractive prices, at this astonishingly low valuation for the entire company! Nor would the stock contain the extraordinary potential on the upside that it has.

In a sense, some of the best opportunities are in the stocks that the financial periodicals knock. Someone once pointed out to me that a leading weekly financial newspaper had been urging short sales and knocking Resorts International shares as the stock price continued to climb rapidly. As late as 1986, this newspaper wrote an article aggressively criticizing Resorts International's accounting practices. Afterward, Resorts International did drop, but then rose again, almost doubling. Only later did the company's stock price suffer because of the excessive debt it incurred in a leveraged buyout. Had you invested and sold at the right time—and there was a long period during which you would have had the opportunity to sell—you would have been a huge winner.

That is the job of these journals—to deliver cynically provocative articles. It makes for interesting reading. It's good copy; it's how they get their readership. To be fair, once in a while, they do a service to the public by knocking something that is really terrible. But they can do a disservice, too, by knocking at an early stage a stock that ultimately shows tremendous merit—an evolving company that hasn't yet proven itself.

Of course, there are lots of negatives with emerging companies. There is no assurance that a new company's product will work. The disclaimers we put in prospectuses and annual reports spell out these factors—that the established, big companies have more financial resources, more human resources, and better access to scientific equipment than newly founded entrepreneurial enterprises.

Rarely can an investor simply relax and sleep peacefully with these potentially explosive winners, because they are so vulnerable to negative press reports, to the sharp drops that pull them down before they can get up and grow into one of the future's leading companies.

A great lesson can be learned from the story of the young man who answered the classified advertisement "Opportunity of a Lifetime" and found himself in the presence of his potential employer, a nervous individual.

"What I am looking for is somebody to do all my worrying," he explained. "Your job will be to shoulder all my cares."

"That's some job, how much do I get?" asked the applicant.

"You get $200,000 a year to make every worry of mine your own," replied the overwrought fellow.

"Where is the $200,000 coming from?" the young man asked.

"Ah, that's your first worry!"

HANG IN THERE

As an investor in emerging companies and/or technology you can't be intimidated by negative press reports or bad experiences. Other less daring investors shun emerging growth stocks because of their unproven record, but you must look at them as opportunities.

Once a growth stock is a proven company, other investors will buy into it, but by then you will have made a big gain in your position—and the stock price will start to decline or even drop precipitously. Before Genentech's major product actually received FDA approval and even reached the market, the stock soared. Once it achieved sales and earnings, the stock came down. After all, expectations and dreams always exceed reality. Multiples occasionally get way up into the clouds. There is a tendency to exaggerate a remote possibility, to magnify the effect of a single event.

As with individual companies, it is important to persevere through industry fluctuations. For example, in January 1992, the Chicago Board of Options Exchange (CBOE) Biotech Index hit a high. The decline that followed, however, precipitated doubt generating an extended period of selling. Ultimately, the index reached a two-year low in July 1994. I knew that the biotech industry still carried the tremendous potential for success and growth as it had before. With stock prices so low and downside risk minimal, I also knew it was a prime time to buy undervalued stocks. By year-end 1995, the CBOE Biotech Index rose by 103 percent! My calculated prediction had come to fruition—the biotech industry and the companies' stocks related to it were in the running again and even more powerfully than we could have anticipated.

PERFECTLY IMPERFECT

Most people who bought Polaroid early bought it for entirely the wrong reason. They bought it because it was the first to develop 3-D glasses for 3-D movies. *House of Wax,* starring Vincent Price, was the first 3-D movie. Moviegoers wore Polaroid paper glasses given out free with the price of admission. This was some time back, before Polaroid was an established company. Polaroid's real breakthrough, of course, was the instant camera—which, ironically and as usual with new, unaccepted technology, was not much appreciated at first. It was almost universally maligned as merely a silly gimmick that would never attain any real consumer interest.

These are the opportunities. When nobody liked the company, Jack Dreyfus—founder of the Dreyfus Fund—built a large part of his fortune and his reputation on Polaroid by staying on top of it and recognizing that it was an important breakthrough and that there would be a good, indeed a great market there.

Biases and defects in judgment make the stock market a most inefficient pricing mechanism. It is widely believed and often argued that the market is a model of perfect rationality at all times. Presumably, the prices are perfect because they digest, reflect, and return to you all the information that's out there. They select values rationally.

Yet I have found that this presumption of rationality is not the best basis on which to make investment decisions. On the contrary, at the very extreme of contagious enthusiasm is when you must get out of the market and sell your stock. When everybody believes a company is terrific. When it draws even pros. When everybody is making money and they are sure the stock is a winner. When it looks to be a sure thing—that's when it's time for you to get out.

NO PAIN, NO GAIN

The willpower needed for this game is considerable, but so is the potential for gains. And that is really what it is all about. It takes backbone to stay with these risk situations. It takes sleepless nights and, at times, seemingly intolerable aggravation. All of us have periods when our performance is less than brilliant. But if we hang in there, during the bad times, then we'll all pull through and enjoy the gratifying rewards. I say: Learn the facts, understand the risks, and act.

The facts substantiate that small companies give big rewards and big companies provide small rewards.

Paradoxically, all the statistics show that there is safety in risk and risk in safety. Safe, secure bonds that allowed one to worry least gave the very poorest returns. Small-cap stocks, at the time they were invested in and during the period they were held, generated anxiety and concern and even sleepless nights and harrowing days—still these are the ones that delivered the best gains.

So play it smart, not safe. Tolerate greater pain and realize the bigger gains.

TEN REASONS YOU SHOULD INVEST
IN SMALL COMPANIES

In summary, therefore, here are ten reasons why I believe in the power of small companies to take a small idea and create a very big profit:

1. The greatest percentage appreciation comes when you invest in a company at a very early stage—start-up or just beyond—before the company achieves meaningful sales and earnings.

2. Because successful small companies can grow rapidly, the stock price may go up by multiples of the initial buying price. It is not unusual for a small company's stock value to triple, quadruple, or multiply even more as it grows, although such a move in a major corporation stock is rare. The returns from investing in small companies over any long-term investment period far exceed the returns on the Dow Jones or any of the other indices of large companies.

3. Small companies, once they get out of the gate and achieve an initial foothold—new products, sales, etc.—are often attractive acquisitions for large companies at a substantial price.

4. It's far more exciting and more fun to invest in small new companies because your investment makes a difference. It actually serves to trigger the company's launch, and you can follow its tangible progress as it hires people, does research, develops new products and services, realizes actual sales and then dramatic growth, and finally achieves bottom-line earnings and recognition as a winner.

5. Your investment is true capitalism. It immediately provides new jobs and the purchase of new capital equipment. Small companies are net hirers.

6. Small companies, historically, are responsible for the development of a disproportionately large portion of the new and exciting products and technologies that promise to positively affect the quality of your life and the lives of your children and grandchildren.

7. The very search and location for an investment in small companies is an exciting adventure and produces a much greater sense of gratification when one succeeds, as compared to investing in a large company or just looking for ongoing dividends.

8. You can get to know the management and actually follow the company's progress as if it were your very own business, with all the exciting highs and lows that such an unfolding investment adventure provides.

9. Small businesses cover the entire range of human activity, thus allowing an investor to focus his investment activities in a field in which he or she has a particular expertise, such as computer peripherals or specific goals, such as medical research or halting or reversing the aging process.

10. Over time, a balanced, diversified portfolio of carefully researched, properly financed, high-risk, potentially high-reward growth companies will outperform a stock portfolio of more mature companies.

End of Chpt. 4

Chpt. 5 > goes to pg. 52 = 6 pgs..

FIVE

THE PRICE IS RIGHT

As the naïve underwriter once said to the greedy entrepreneur, "I have good news and bad news. The good news is we're bringing your new issue out at a very high price. The bad news is no one wants to buy it."

If you're investing in a new company, be sure that the underwriter—the brokerage company that's bringing out the issue—cares about correctly pricing the initial public offering.

In so many Wall Street firms, an executive or some vice president does the deal. But their reputation—and the firm's—is not on the line. Once they raise the funds, they get a commission. The firm sells the company to the public for whatever the market will bear and collects its fees. For them it's just another piece of business.

My motivations are different. I get personally involved in my underwritings. I am proud of my reputation and that of my firm and I want to preserve the prestige that we worked so hard to achieve. I would rather lose an issue if I feel that it isn't priced appropriately than bring it out at the wrong price. I fight hard defending that position.

If it were up to me, all those vice presidents on the Street, the individuals who price the IPOs and all firms on the Street that do public offerings, would be required to buy a meaningful amount of stock with their own money at the offering price. Then they would care. If they were part of the group that takes a high risk hoping for commensurately high returns, then they, too, would price companies accordingly.

I represent the risk taker, the men and women who put up their hard-earned money to fund a new company's business, and I take pains to protect these investors. They put up the risk capital. They supply the wherewithal to implement entrepreneurial dreams and aspirations. And if a company succeeds, they deserve a big reward. Because if it doesn't, they stand to lose a lot of money.

My main concern is to price a company well so that I give the venturesome, risk-taking investor a good deal.

This is not a matter of altruism. The one tenet central to my business is this: We are only as good as the performance of our last two or three issues.

I price a company so attractively that I am willing and anxious to put my own money into it—to put my money where my mouth is. That is the key, because in the last analysis, if nobody else will buy it, then I will buy it myself. I know that if I believe enough in the company we're bringing public and in the fact that I am pricing it fairly, I will put my own money, my family's money, anybody's money, into that company. And I do.

THE VALUE OF UNDERVALUING

I always urge entrepreneurs to underprice their issue. Because when its first public offering is successful, a company develops a following right at the outset. Its investors are happy and its stock moves up. Later, if it approaches the market again, it can easily raise more capital. Moreover, once a company is a winner, it feeds on itself. It does well, and then when the insiders want to sell some of their stock, they'll find a ready market for it at a very good price.

If a stock is overvalued, the founders or venture capitalists may be ecstatic on the first day. But a year later, when it is selling at a fraction of its offering price—and that is where they sell their stock—their euphoria will be gone. I urge people to price their deal at whatever is reasonable and fair, even better than fair.

If it's priced high, the first day you may get excited about how rich you are. But then when it drops and fades away you're not really rich. You don't want—you *shouldn't* want—a quick momentary thrill. Don't go for the instant gratification of the sudden but unsustainable high price of that first day. What you want is a rise in the aftermarket. That's when it really counts. Think of the long run—when you are happy because the stock went up and you are truly richer.

Underprice it!

Then, when your stock starts to perform, because of the momentum you'll be able to sell what was initially a $4 or $5 stock for perhaps $24 or $25.

For me the client is the investor, the person who takes the risk every day and puts up the funds. He is the one I go back to again and again as I attempt to bring out each new company.

The proof of the pudding is in the tasting.

The markets periodically go through boom periods where there is more and more money coming into the new issue market. This results in investors aggressively looking for investment opportunities. Generally at the early stage of the new "up" cycle, the deals are scarce. There is an excess amount of capital chasing too few deals. So the new issues run up.

Many of these companies do not deserve funding. They are funded, however, because the money is there for them. Underwriters compete against each other for a limited number of deals, bidding up the price at which they are willing to value the companies, unfortunately producing too many overpriced issues.

Ultimately, when reality sets in, prices come down, and marginal companies that shouldn't have been underwritten fail to perform to expectations or go under completely.

When a stock is overpriced it has only one place to go—down.

If the overpricing of deals becomes habitual, as it often does, then the whole new issue market is negatively affected. Finally, the individual investor abandons this market, making it almost impossible to raise capital for new companies, even very good ones.

Whether it's an individual or an institutional investor, if they experience a loss in one new issue and then a second and finally a third, when you call them to invest in the next IPO they will respond, "No thanks." Buyers dry up and the game is over—at least until underwriters once again price IPOs so attractively that they are irresistible and the new issue market revives and a new cycle begins.

In all my years I've never met any client we took public who complained that his shares rose too much the first day or the first month. They are always elated when their shares go up in price and so, of course, are our venturesome and deserving investors.

Almost every time I fight with a client opposed to my thinking on pricing, and I reluctantly give in and bring it out at a somewhat higher price than I think appropriate, it proves to be a mistake.

In 95 percent of the cases, we both lose, the entrepreneur is unhappy because the stock went down, as I warned him, and I am unhappy because our valued investors lost money and our track record performance is temporarily tarnished.

In most other cases, where I price a deal as I judge appropriate— even if the owners thought it was low and only went along reluctantly—they are happy later when it does well.

When it turns into a winner in the aftermarket, I never get complaints that I underpriced a company.

SOLOMON'S BABY

There is a basic conflict between the entrepreneur and the investor. I represent them both and must do right by them. In a way, I act as arbitrator and often it requires the wisdom of Solomon. The entrepreneur-client asks, "How shall I price my company? What is fair? What do you recommend?" At the same time, I also represent the investor-client who is not present at that pricing meeting. I have to find the perfect solution suitable to them both.

If a company comes out at $6 and goes to $150, no one ever comes back to me to say, "Gee whiz, you priced it too low." The people at Home Shopping Network (HSN), to the best of my knowledge, never complained to Merrill Lynch when the stock went from $37 to as high as $133 in less than five months. They were elated.

The initial price of HSN was the tip of an iceberg that they correctly gave away at a bargain price. The lower price drove demand, which ultimately drove prices up. The higher price then made the stock a stronger acquisition currency. That's what made the whole iceberg more valuable. Then they used their rather high-priced stock to make acquisitions of other good companies. The founding entrepreneurs were major beneficiaries.

When we make a good pricing decision, everybody is a winner. The investor, the risk taker who funds these companies, wins too. The venture capitalist, the entrepreneur whose stock is doing well, also wins. A stock price that is doing well is how one should value one's wealth. Then if they need to raise additional money, they can issue new stock at the higher price. We, as the underwriters, win. A win is what we try to design.

Sometimes it's a tough job selling to my entrepreneur clients. Almost invariably, I advise them to price their company at several million dollars less than what one of my competitors might be promising them. Clients come in and say, "So-and-so offered me more." I say, "Well, take it if you think that is crucial. I'm designing a deal that I think works well for you. In the long run you'll be better off taking mine." I don't have to do every deal.

When everybody is bidding up IPO deals to outrageous numbers and valuations, I turn down more deals than ever. Exaggerated pricing means that the public will buy anything. When that happens, we're really close to the end of a stock market cycle and we will all get hurt.

There were years when we saw an enormous bull market in new issues. We would bring something out at $5 a share and it would open at $10 and go immediately to $15 or $20. Things shouldn't happen so fast and certainly not for every issue, as it did in those years. Not surprisingly, the bottom soon fell out.

One of the reasons venture capitalists form companies is to seed them for a year or two with a view to taking them public. If under-writers kill the public market by overpricing new issues, then the venture capitalists become less interested in sinking new money into start-ups. In fact, if they can't liquidate some of their holdings through the IPO marketplace, they quickly withdraw from funding other deserving new ventures. Venture capitalists find it hard enough saving the companies that they're already invested in, which may often need mezzanine financing (that is, financing provided in tiers over time).

Chpt. 6 > goes to pg. 59 = 7 pgs.

SIX

CAPITAL STEPS

Of all the activities on Wall Street, the one I find most magical and rewarding is investing in young companies and taking them public. The most money can be made by both investors and entrepreneurs in a start-up company that builds itself from the very early stages where it is just an idea to the point where it is producing new, exciting products and significant revenues and is becoming profitable.

Bringing a company to that stage is the most difficult thing to achieve in an investment; however, that is where the greatest increment in value is realized—particularly when you start from a zero base and finally generate meaningful revenues and/or profits. Wall Street then sits up and takes notice because the rise is so steep and the stock really flies.

By nature, investors—even sophisticated analysts—generally take this posture: "My G-d!" they say. "This company went from zero to $5 million in two years." Extrapolating from that performance, they say, "In two more years, it will be doing $20 million; then in four years, it will be doing $80 million." They anticipate future performance and begin paying for that growth. When Wall Street "discounts" the future, stocks sell at their highest multiples. That is also when early-stage investors make their greatest percentage gains.

In other words, by the time it actually happens and when a company realizes its goal and promise, the stock doesn't sell at nearly the exciting price it did when it was still a dream.

This is typical of many development-stage companies that we

choose to fund. Their shares will often trade substantially higher than the original offering price because of improving progress, technological milestones, the expectations of the market, and security analysis about the revenue and earnings potential for the company.

However, there can be times when, because of competition, obsolescence, or simply stock market conditions, share prices come down. What we stress is to be invested at a very early stage, when both the risk-reward ratio as well as the dream are very exciting. This, historically, is where the greatest returns can be made.

Start up with Start-ups

My method for becoming rich is buying start-up companies or companies still in their earliest development stages. The greatest rewards lie in these companies because they offer astronomical potential returns—tenfold (1,000 percent) or twenty times (2,000 percent) on your investment or the far from uncommon rapid gain of 50 percent to 300 percent. You just don't find that—at least not very often—on the Big Board.

Before going any further, let's recognize and discuss the risk-reward ratio. The greatest rewards are related to the greatest risks. The greatest risks lie in these kinds of companies because they can become total failures. Many may never generate sales or earnings, just management's optimistic projections and vision of what the company can one day achieve.

That is the reason we bet on the jockey. I refer to management as the jockey because the entrepreneur, the founder of the company, is the person who holds the reins, gives direction to the company, and gives it their all, taking the company to the winner's circle.

We look for certain ingredients in the jockey and that is what we buy. We can't predict the future. What we are underwriting or financing is essentially a person who we believe is great and that person's dream. We like to find a dream whose time has come: the first videocassette company; the first genetics company; the first super-conductivity company; one of the first cellular phone companies; or an unusual database or software company.

We underwrote perhaps the first videocassette company, Teltronics, later renamed Video Corporation of America, for which we raised several million dollars in 1971. It is worth several hundred million dollars today.

We help make entrepreneurs' aspirations and dreams happen. If they do, the investors, the risk takers, and the venture capitalists (in our case, public venture capitalists—our investors) all get rich. It's a great feeling.

PUBLIC VENTURE CAPITALIST

Earlier in modern American history, only the privileged few—families such as the Rockefellers, Whitneys, and Carnegies, who, generations ago, possessed enough capital—were the only people with the opportunity to invest in promising start-up companies at the earliest stage. Only they could act as venture capitalists and put millions of dollars into young enterprises that might blossom into any of the large industrial successes of their era.

These venturesome risk takers provided early entrepreneurs with capital. They set up companies and helped the entrepreneurs build the business for a year or two. They then brought these companies to their friends on Wall Street (the Morgan Stanleys and the Rothschilds) to do the public underwritings, selling shares to the public at large. At the very first public offering, the venture capitalists got back a high-multiple return on their original investment.

The general public, historically, never participated in the massive investments that private venture capital requires. Our philosophy is exactly the opposite. We went to the same creative entrepreneurs and took them public at the earliest stage of their company's life, involving smaller investors at precisely the same early point as once drew the successful venture capitalists. Then, with much smaller investments, the public could participate and, hopefully, experience the same kind of high return.

We give this kind of opportunity to our sophisticated, aggressive investors on a consistent basis. These individual investors lack the ability to invest the $5 million that might fund a venture-stage company but could comfortably participate in a $10,000, $50,000, or $100,000 position in an underwriting of that company.

Every day we establish opportunities for general investors to be "Rockefellers," investing in these same types of exciting, pioneering companies in which risks are matched with equally high rewards when the company proves successful.

Most of our greatest success stories show the validity of this concept. Our track record proves that we opened to the public an enormous potential for gains previously unavailable to them. We, in effect, democratized venture capitalism.

LOOKING FOR LIQUIDITY

In some respects, public venture capital situations are a better investment than private placements because they offer more liquidity.

With private venture capital, you're involved in private placements with no public market. If you want to sell, you must find someone to purchase your investment in a private transaction. The Rockefellers locked their funds up until their companies went public. Until then, they had no liquidity.

With public venture capital investments, if you want to sell, whether to lock in your profit or minimize your loss, you can liquidate your position because a market exists. You may not always get the best price for your stock, but you can get out and protect yourself, as well as realize the offsetting benefit of a tax loss. On the other hand, if you hold and if the stock has a big move, your profits can be of a magnitude unparalleled elsewhere.

The liquidity of public venture capital is a significant advantage, something like the difference between owning real estate and owning stock. If you own real estate, you can sell your property, but you've got to find a real estate broker and a buyer. Sometimes, if you get lucky, the broker can sell fairly quickly. Sometimes you may sit for a year or longer before you find an appropriate buyer.

With the stock market, even though you may not always like the price, you can call up your broker at any time and sell. You need not wait until your private company finally goes public—if indeed it ever does—to find a market for these locked-in investments. On any particular day, for any particular reason, you can sell.

A WAY OUT

A story is told about a commercial flight that got into trouble. When one of the engines caught fire, the captain calmly reassured the passengers that the fire would soon be out. A second engine burst into flames and once again the captain spoke to the passengers reassuringly. Suddenly a third engine was ablaze. After a few moments the captain headed toward the exit with a parachute on his back and calmly said to the passengers, "Don't anyone panic, I'm going for help." And out he jumped.

Liquidity is worth a lot. You can always bail out.

Ironically, by taking advantage of this liquidity, you may be selling the baby, the infant company, before it develops into the mature adult you hope it will be. Some people will buy stock in a company at $6 per share. If it goes up to $8 per share, they'll say, "That's a big profit. I made 33 percent in four days." Or: "It's up a point, over 16 percent. That's over 1,400 percent annualized. That's stratospheric!" Then they sell and miss the really big move.

We had such a situation with Nova Pharmaceuticals. In 1983, Nova came out in units of $6.25. In a month it rose to $8, but you could have bought all you wanted for $6.50 or less during that first year. Then, within three years, the units hit a high of $187!

Some found it rewarding to get out quickly with a 25 percent profit in a month. But those who were patient and rode it to $187, or anywhere near, did much better. They made the returns that savvy venture capitalists seek.

One of the requirements for investing in these young, emerging companies is recognizing that you are buying an infant who must first crawl, then walk, and then run before it can reach for the mountaintops. It may stumble along the way. You want to hold for that expectation, for the time when the company moves into a dramatic growth pattern that the market then extrapolates into the future—and pays for that extrapolation now.

Some actual cases are the best evidence. A few years ago, we took a company public called the Daxor Corporation, run by Dr. Joseph Feldshuh.

Daxor stored semen. People store semen for various reasons. A man with cancer might store his semen so that he can produce offspring even after radiation renders him sterile. Women wanting artificial insemination often go to a semen bank. For whatever reason, there is a market for it.

We did a public offering for Daxor at $7 a unit. For a year the stock did not perform well. In fact, it tumbled to $4.50 soon after the offering. That can and will happen. A young company just starting out lacks a performance record, so investor interest can be minimal and trading thin.

It stayed at about $5.00 for two years. Then, in early 1987, after languishing at that level it soared in one month to $37. Since it also had an accompanying warrant, the unit that included the shares and warrant moved up a total of almost $50. Something that cost $7 at the offering and went to $4.50 because nobody liked it when it came out, multiplied over seven times.

In this case, the stock benefited from discovery and recognition, as stocks tend to do.

It was a belated recognition, real or imagined, based on the company's involvement with AIDS. Daxor stores frozen blood as well as semen and, at the time, people were nervous about blood transfusions from others because of the AIDS panic. It was believed that many families would freeze their blood, creating personal blood banks when they needed it.

I don't know if that is really a major development or not. But because some institutions became interested and excited by the *perception* of a major development, Daxor started trading tens and even hundreds of thousands of shares a day. Almost three years after we did the offering, somebody discovered the company and it did phenomenally well.

These are the opportunities that arise from entrepreneurial situations when they work. The maximum downside of this unit that we brought out at $7 was 7 points. And although it did go down temporarily to a low of $4.50, the most its IPO investors could lose was $7 for each unit purchased! But the upside potential was many times that price.

End of Chpt 6

chpt. 7) gres to pg. 73 = 13 pgs

SEVEN

STARTING A NEW COMPANY

Being an entrepreneur or the founder of a company is certainly one way of becoming a millionaire quickly. Some people I backed in the past were just men or women with new ideas who became not millionaires, but multimillionaires, while still in their twenties.

Because I specialize in this niche of funding emerging growth companies from their inception, more entrepreneurial, creative people, whom I call "the jockeys," come to us. We once looked for them; now, they look for us.

The entrepreneur wants a successful company, which meshes with the investor's desire to invest when we find the jockey capable of taking a new company from a point where it is worth little to the point where it can realize its economic potential. Through our new-issue investors we provide the wherewithal, the risk capital, and the funds that can make this miracle happen.

CHOOSING THE COMPANY

The sales manager of a dog food company once asked his salespeople how they liked the company's new advertising program. "Great! Best in the business!"

"How do you like our new label and package?"

"Great! Best in the business!"

"How do you like our sales force?"

They were the sales force. They knew they were good.

"OK, then, so we've got the best label, the best package, and the best advertising program being sold by the best sales force in the business. Tell me why we are in seventeenth place in the dog food business?"

The room fell silent.

Finally, one of them got up and said, "It's the damn dogs . . . they won't eat the stuff!"

So the first thing I look for is a good product, a good business idea—an idea whose time has come. Is the world in need of this product? Is it ready for it? Is the product exciting, like a cure for heart disease or cancer, or something that grows hair on your head? Is it an aphrodisiac, a cheap alternative energy source, a new way of enhancing productivity or cleaning up hazardous waste?

We have all types of needs as a society for our health, communication, and infrastructure. There are products and services that can make all our lives better. If someone comes along with an idea that can fill a human need, I want to back it.

The next thing I look for is a good business plan—one that is both well prepared and on the right track. I won't see the principals until they send in such a plan. The business plan is essential because it's the first "salesman" sent through the door. Unless the entrepreneurs are smart enough to send in a well-prepared and carefully thought-out business plan, I won't meet them.

People call me fifty times a day and say they have a fabulous company or a fabulous idea. I say, "Great. I don't want to waste your time or mine unless it meets certain thresholds, so send me a business plan. If I do have a threshold interest, I'll set up a meeting right away. If it looks as if it makes sense and if you're ready to do it at a price that's attractive to the public, then we will really move and raise the money you need to implement its successful fruition."

The plan must demonstrate intelligence. Sometimes I get a business plan that introduces what the Harvard Business School calls "insignificant numbers." What do I mean by that? The business plan includes projections. Projections are essential. They tell us what future revenues and earnings the entrepreneur sees for the company and for himself and we want them to be big. But if he projects sales of $1,935,000.42 for the first year and says, "In the fifth year, I'll do $27,946,000.88," down to the last penny, those are insignificant numbers and I know the guy is inept.

If he is right about the $27 million five years out, which is a gross number, that alone would be a miracle. But when he extends his projections—which are at best an intelligent estimate—to the last digit and puts down the 42 cents or the 88 cents, what he has specified is so irrelevant, so insignificant, so implausibly precise, it means he just ran the numbers through a computer. It shows he wasn't thinking or didn't even take the time to carefully review what he was submitting.

BIG PLANS, BIG BUCKS

The plan must be ambitious. We must know the entrepreneurs' goals for the company. If they aren't exciting, we will not underwrite it. We want someone who dreams about being listed on the New York Stock Exchange and about building a major company—a Fortune 500 company. We want a potentially big winner.

If an entrepreneur says, "I'll make $50,000 the first year, $70,000 the second year, and $95,000 the third year," we tell him "Great! That's a good business. But that's a good, private business. Keep it and build it and lots of luck."

But if realistic projections—based on research, market comparisons, and a strong idea—tell us they will make $1 million in profits the second year, $5 million in profits the third year, and $25 million in the fifth year, then we get into it because even if the entrepreneur is only partly right, if they only get part of the way there, it is still a potentially very exciting vehicle. If the entrepreneur says, "I need $5 million or $6 million to make it work," that is a reasonable capital risk for a potentially exciting return.

If we put in $6 million for half this company, setting a $12 million-postfinancing valuation on it, and four years out it is doing $50 million in revenues and growing, that kind of dramatic growth may set a $500-million valuation for the company on the public market. If the public investors have put up $6 million dollars for half of that, they have an exciting return.

The $6 million could be worth $250 million. More than forty times the venture investment, that's what we are striving for.

Having determined that the business plan is sufficiently ambitious and exciting, I need to be sure it's realistic. If the founders say, "We will build a great business, but it will cost us $200 million," I don't even bother meeting with them. They may be entitled to it, but it's not in our ballpark. The risk we run on $200 million is not the same as on $6 million. Turning $200 million into $2 billion or $3 billion is much harder than turning $6 million into $100 million or $200 million.

Bet on the Jockey

Once I've determined that the business plan is exciting, meets a need, and offers a product whose time we think is now, I look for the brilliance and innovation of the jockey.

I do that through conversation, cross-examination, background search, and by evaluating whatever the entrepreneur's resume and career tell me about him or her. More fundamentally, it comes from my long experience and interaction with people.

It comes from focusing on the best qualities and recognizing outstanding traits.

This is illustrated by the story of the two men who were in a dispute over whose horse belonged to whom. They decided to go before the town's wise man.

"We can't tell our horses apart. What can we do?" the two men asked.

The wise man thought about it and said, "You let your horse's mane grow long and you cut your horse's mane short. Then, yours will be the one with the long mane and yours will be the one with the short mane."

The two men were very pleased but a month later they were back complaining that the second horse's mane had grown long and again the two horses couldn't be differentiated.

The wise man gave it some thought and said, "You let your horse's tail grow long and you cut your horse's tail short, then yours will be the one with the long tail and yours will be the one with the short tail."

The two men were pleased. But a month later they were back again, complaining that the tail of the second horse had grown and the horses were again indistinguishable from each other.

The wise man thought and thought. After an extended period of deep thought he suddenly announced, "I have it! Yours is the white horse and yours is the black one!"

Detecting the distinguishing traits that make a winner is essential. Usually, they're right under your nose, which often makes them hard to detect. So if your nose doesn't know, use your common sense.

All sorts of things in the business plan give me clues. I go through the background of the people to see what they have done—what interesting or intriguing accomplishments exhibit the ingredients I seek. Have they run successful businesses before?

We'll sometimes do an offering just because the person coming to us built a business from scratch, sold it for millions or even hundreds of millions of dollars, and is now starting a new company. Any entrepreneur who did it before is worth betting on again. There's a chance they may not do it again, but at least they demonstrated the knowledge and drive to do it once.

If I got fired tomorrow and started from zero again, it would take hard work, but I would be back on top because I know how it's done. So I bet on the winning jockeys.

Even if these entrepreneurs don't turn a small company into a major company, but just get it off the ground and make it work, some big, established firm will likely come along and buy them out. Large companies find starting an operation or new business much more expensive than buying one outright. Large companies confront high costs and a low success ratio in dealing with new ideas, because of their institutional risk aversion.

Young companies take on new enterprises far more readily. That's why they sell at a high price in relation to their sales or earnings or any other actual results. They start up and get their projects off the ground with tremendous energy and with high expectations of being meaningful, if not major, factors in the market.

We look for people who are gutsy, who show the tenacity not only to write a good business plan, but to push us to do the deal. We often see as many as one hundred business plans a week and probably on average forty a week. We underwrite only a handful. There are millions of people with ideas, but the best ones take the idea and then move on it. They are smart enough to find us or somebody like us to help them make it happen.

THE BIG FOUR

When I say that I bet on the jockey, I mean that I look for the leader who will make money for the company and all its investors. I look for four qualities: mental brilliance, adaptability, decisiveness, and a neurotic drive to win big.

After thirty years of meeting with thousands of people who run companies or start them, detecting these attributes is second nature.

I still make mistakes, of course. I may choose good people yet make a mistake in timing. I underwrote an exciting oil service company, Accutest, in the early 1980s. Accutest signed contracts with Exxon, the biggest oil company of them all, but then the oil business crashed and the company lost all its contracts. The people were good and put the right products in place, but the company went under. A classic case of the right people in the right company at the wrong time.

"Adapt-ability"

Although adaptability couldn't save Accutest, that's a trait I want to see in jockeys. Brilliance will only carry you so far without your being adaptive.

The ears and eyes must be open. By changing and making mid-course corrections, entrepreneurs will manage the money we give them to better ends. They'll survive most setbacks.

A classic case of adaptability was exemplified by J. Paul Getty. His first investment in oil exploration turned out to be a dry well and he was devastated. He was ready to kill himself when he got a brilliant insight. He sold the wells—to his mother!

You knew then that he would be the richest man in America.

Although I disapprove of his tactics, they demonstrate in the extreme a determination, an ability to roll with the punches, and the creativity to come out ahead even when things go against you.

Some entrepreneurs made money for us for the wrong reasons. Five years later, you wouldn't recognize the success of their companies vis-à-vis the original plan, because they recognized necessary changes and moved into other areas. One company was practically wiped out. Its stock collapsed to 6 cents a share.

However, management was adaptable. They were mathematical whizzes and came up with a new product that didn't cost them all that much to develop. In two years, the stock was up to $35 a share. That's what I mean by adaptable. The original business we funded for them flopped—hard.

But by being adaptable, they mobilized their people and resources and made the company work. I did this with my own company. I moved into different areas over time and developed new kinds of success.

A TRUE OLYMPIAN

Don Panoz is one of my favorite jockeys of all time. I really love the guy! His NYSE company, Élan Corporation, demonstrated what may be the most dramatic earnings growth record in American capitalism's history. It set a record, for companies followed by Standard & Poor, with four successive years of 100 percent or better profit growth. Wow! And Élan's shares rose from our initial offering price—adjusted for splits—of 91 cents per share in 1982 to a price in July 1997 of $49.87 per share.

Panoz, born and raised in West Virginia, is just like you or me. Maybe just a little more imaginative—a dreamer and a doer. He was in the pharmaceutical industry before starting Élan in Ireland (with satellite offices in Gainesville, Georgia). To this very day, he tells me that I spent most of our first meeting talking on the phone and doing trades. But notwithstanding that, he apparently impressed me enough that we gave him a letter of intent to raise $4,375,000 for his start-up company.

Before we filed his prospectus our lawyer advised me that Panoz was piloting his own plane overseas all alone—a little plane that you could blow over if you breathed on it too hard.

I said, "Tell Don two things. One, I won't underwrite any company that has its own plane, and especially not a start-up that needs every penny it can lay its hands on to ensure that the company will have a chance to succeed. And two, I particularly won't underwrite and finance a company where the jockey I bet on is flying solo over the ocean to Ireland in a tiny plane." My lawyer conveyed an even simpler message to Panoz: "Either dispose of the plane or we back out of the deal."

Don sold the plane and we launched his company. It took off and never stopped flying.

Élan's market cap value exceeded $3.5 billion in 1997 and it is one of the leading employers in all of Ireland with its shares listed in Ireland and Britain, as well as New York.

About a year after we took Don's company public, I heard that Don bought some acreage outside Atlanta and was growing grapes and producing wine.

I must confess, when I heard that I thought we backed a true eccentric. After all, who grew grapes and produced wine in Georgia? It was crazy.

Today Château Élan is one of the most beautiful, most successful wineries in all America. Inside that beautiful château is a magnificent, shiny, immaculate aluminum winery, a wine museum that portrays in murals and displays the history of wine making. There are two superb, first-class restaurants and a charming shopping mart that attracts hundreds of thousands of visitors a year. Moreover, Château Élan regularly wins national and international prizes for the quality and superiority of its wines. In addition, Panoz built two outstanding golf courses and a four-star hotel and corporate conference center.

Don Panoz is a true genius. He built Château Élan at the same time as he built one of the greatest American companies of the last decade. And yet, if you meet him, you immediately recognize that he's a regular guy just like you or me. But he is a guy with a vision and a dream, and he worked at it. His dedication and perseverance turned a regular guy into a multimillionaire—an accomplished, truly productive genius. If a regular guy like Don Panoz can do it, so can you. Get yourself a pair of boots, visualize the dream, and start today with imagination, dedication, and hard work. Someday, someone will be writing about you just as I am now writing about Don Panoz, an entrepreneurial hero.

MOVE ON A DIME

Another quality I look for is decisiveness. I want jockeys who make decisions. Today—*now*—not next month. When an entrepreneur gets through with a meeting and says to me, "I'll go back and discuss this with my board of directors," I say, "I'm not interested in doing business with you," even if I am impressed with their business plan.

The entrepreneur is shocked.

"What are you talking about?" they say.

"There is only one thing, one advantage, that a small company has going for it over a big company," I'll say. "Big companies have more financial resources, more human resources, more bank connections, more salespeople, more personnel, more research clout. Anything you can think of, big companies have more. The only thing they don't have that a small company has is the ability to make a fast decision."

A small company with a decisive leader can move on a dime. By the time the big companies decide to do market research and bring out a product, young companies are already in production, carving out market share.

In a way, that is the greatness of my company. We'll complete an underwriting before some of my Wall Street counterparts can get past their research desks.

In other words, we'll make the decision at the first meeting and get our lawyers in the process of filing with the Securities and Exchange Commission (SEC). We will rush our timing to stay ahead in a good market. We'll go through the gestation period, go public, and turn the funds over to the company so it can get moving, before some larger investment bankers are halfway through their decision-making process.

HEALTHY NEUROTICISM

Finally, I want jockeys who are neurotic. By that, I mean I want them to desire to be the biggest and the best. The problem with success is that its formula is the same as the one for ulcers. But I'm looking for people with a compulsive, unrelenting inner drive to be successful, because then I know that they will work—as I do—one hundred hours a week. If necessary, they will meet in the middle of the night. They will fly anywhere, any time, to get an order. Their need to be successful, their dreams and their aspirations, are so predominant that they will break their necks for themselves and, as a byproduct, make winners out of our investors.

I don't know that I would want my daughters to marry one of these guys, because in a sense they're only married to the business. But they are neurotic in a way that is healthy by our "success model" standards.

Let me give you an example of what I mean. Two entrepreneurs come to my office within a week of each other. The first showed sales of $5 million one year, $5.2 million the next year, and $5.4 million the year after that. His was a new product and one about to explode. But I say, "I'd have to bet against you. You'll never do it." He is insulted and he asks me why I feel that way.

"Because," I say, "your track record says that not only haven't you grown, you haven't even kept up with the rate of inflation with your sales and earnings. Why would I believe that tomorrow you're going to explode? I have to buy the track record. Once in a while I may be wrong. An entrepreneur can turn out to be different from his past and suddenly explode. But right now, I'd bet against you."

"Look," he says. "My business is about to explode, but I've been having trouble with my wife. We were going to get divorced, but I've been busy working to reconcile my marriage."

"If you can save your marriage, that's wonderful—family is very important. But I'm not going to do a deal with you. You have a set of priorities that I think is very healthy, but your company is not one

I want to finance right now. I don't believe you can make the growth happen. If a guy batted .250 for three years and he tells me he's going to bat .350 this next year, I have to bet against him."

A week later, the second man, this one with a start-up company, comes in. No sales or earnings to show—he is developing a product.

"I work day and night," he says. "I work Sundays. I got to the point where my wife said, 'You gotta stop this.' She gave me an ultimatum: 'It's either me or the business. I can't take it.'

"So," he says, "I divorced her."

I underwrote him and his company in a minute.

Both people wrote good business plans. The man with $5 million in revenues offered as good a plan as the man with the brand-new, unproven product. But the second guy was totally dedicated. We brought out his stock at $2 and it sold as high as $18. He came up with state-of-the-art new products that were thoroughly exciting.

I am not saying that as a human being I appreciate his values. All I am saying is that that kind of drive, that kind of tenacious, compulsive desire to be successful, is important when you're placing bets on jockeys.

UPSIDE DOWN

If the jockeys possess all these ingredients, I back them. And if you buy into one of their companies, the arithmetic works in your favor.

If you put up $6,000 dollars for 1,000 shares, the most you will ever lose is $6,000. And you probably won't lose that much. Some $6 stocks may go up 50 percent to $9. Or 100 percent to $12. Some will do poorly and will fall 50 percent to $3. Perhaps one in twenty will go into bankruptcy. Even then, they'll sell at 25 cents or 50 cents because they still have some residuals or tax losses worth something and people continue trading them in the hope that they can be revived.

And some companies eventually *are* revived. Sometimes they find new arenas. Sometimes they get bought out as shells that let other companies go public without having to file and that may give them a tax loss carry-forward to boot. Worst case, on the downside you lose $6,000.

But if you get one big winner out of a dozen in five years, and it goes from $6 to $100, a multiple of 1,600 percent (sixteen times your initial investment), that $6,000 investment becomes $100,000. The arithmetic works in your favor because the most you can lose is 100 percent on the downside. On the upside you can make 500, 1,000, or 1,600 percent or more!

End of Chpt. 7

II

THE SCHOOL OF HARD KNOCKS

76.

chpt. 8 > goes to pg. 101 = 25 pgs

EIGHT

GROWING UP

My most striking recollection of childhood is how backward and rebellious I was early on. I had only one interest in life—my one love—the Brooklyn Dodgers. School had absolutely no appeal for me.

At yeshiva—a Jewish school providing secular and religious instruction—my teachers, trained in a strict, old-fashioned discipline, beat me up. When I came home, my father, frustrated that I was not doing well in school and disillusioned by the tough life America offered a newly arrived European immigrant, also beat me up. Finally, the non-Jewish neighborhood kids beat me up because I was wearing a yarmulke. For my first fourteen years I thought I was a punching bag.

All in all I didn't find my childhood much fun, to say the least. I went to yeshiva six days a week, Sunday through Friday, from nine in the morning until seven at night, with only a lunch break and a fifteen-minute recess. The only time we were dismissed early was on Fridays so we could prepare for the Sabbath. Today the Sabbath is my favorite day. But as a kid, because of its many restrictions I did not appreciate it. I hated it. I wasn't allowed to play ball or turn on the radio. Worst of all, I couldn't hear or see my beloved Dodger games, which I lived for.

Each day I grew more discontented and as a consequence, I rebelled early.

Rebel with a Cause

After doing poorly my first term in the Brooklyn yeshiva high school, my parents, eager to improve my results, transferred me to a Manhattan yeshiva. Once again, I was absent practically all term. After the term ended, I arranged a transfer back to my old school.

Preparing a letter on stationery that I "borrowed" from the principal's office in the Manhattan school, I meticulously recorded my five courses with passing grades. A friend signed it with an elaborate flourish and brought it to the old school. Actually, I didn't pass anything that term since I hardly ever showed up for any classes.

One day, the principal came into my classroom. He wanted to see my mother. The school figured out that I didn't have a proper transcript and demoted me.

I refused. I rebelled. At fifteen, I dropped out of school. At least I tried.

I was sent to what they called a "continuation school." All I had to do was show up once a week, on Thursday morning, for two hours. Only really "bad" kids dropped out, so practically everyone at this continuation school—other than myself—had a reform school record.

The boys had shivs in their boots. The girls had prostitution records—but I was so naïve I didn't even know what a prostitute was! All I knew was that I was scared out of my mind each time I had to show up and report alongside my new classmates.

Though I was relatively innocent by the hard-core juvenile delinquent standards, I was certainly on my way to full-scale failure. For one thing, at fifteen I could barely read. I wouldn't have read at all except for scouring the sports pages of the *Daily News* every day.

At fifteen, I was a real loser.

DOUBLE TROUBLE

I hung out in poolrooms. There, strangely enough, I learned some of the earliest and best lessons in fundamental financial strategies—strategies that still affect my business decisions.

In the poolroom I watched the bookmakers and the guys who came in and placed bets on sports events. Then I, too, started betting on college basketball games and major league baseball.

My love for the Brooklyn Dodgers continued. While listening to baseball games, I stood in front of the radio and swung an imaginary bat in the air, visualizing a base hit for Dixie Walker. I prayed to G-d for homers for Dolf Camilli. I promised G-d that if Camilli homered, G-d could take my right arm. I constantly made deals with G-d for helping my adored Brooklyn Dodgers; I was that fanatical.

One day came a brilliant insight. I said to myself, "Wow, I'm going to beat the bookies and get rich!" No team ever lost twenty days in a row, I reasoned, or even ten days in a row. Well, hardly ever. So if I bet on a team and doubled my bet every day, sooner or later I would surely be a winner.

I bet on the Dodgers.

In those days, the St. Louis Cardinals were great. Their players included Stan "the Man" Musial, Enos Slaughter, Harry Brecheen, and Howie Pollet. The Dodgers were just on the verge of becoming great. As it happened, the Dodgers and Cardinals met for a three-game series just as I had my revelation. The odds were 2 to 1 for the Cardinals, so a $10 bet on the Dodgers would pay $20.

I said to myself, "I'll bet $10 on Sunday. If I lose I'll double up and bet $20 on Monday. And on Tuesday, I'll double and bet $40. The chances are I can't lose three days in a row."

But I lost all three days.

Then, when the Dodgers first played the Cubs, the odds were 2 to 1 against them—the bookmakers wanted a bet of $10 to get $5. It wasn't a double anymore. Now I had to lay out $160 to win only $80.

The $160 was an astronomical amount of money for me, money

I didn't have. I was only working part-time jobs. I took deposit bottles from my house and returned them for small change. Then I borrowed money from friends, even "borrowing" my mother's precious grocery money.

It took me months and months to work off that debt, but I learned two important lessons that still help me today.

First, never bet emotionally. The only reason I bet on the Dodgers was that I was in love with them. I never rationally analyzed their chances of winning.

In the stock market, you can't get emotional or fall in love with a stock. If you are emotionally involved, you must stay away. You must base your decisions upon sound judgment, superior research, and identification of exceptional opportunities.

Second, I learned the dramatic effect of compounding. For example, if the Indians who sold Manhattan for a mere pittance of $24 had invested that tiny amount at 6 percent compounded interest, it would, amazingly, be worth more than all of Manhattan today!!

In the stock market, even if you begin with a relatively small amount and successfully invest such funds to yield a compounded 25 percent rate of return, your investment will just about double every three years. The growth of wealth you experience will be magnificent and you could quickly become very wealthy. Starting with $25,000 and investing it at 25 percent, after forty-two years you would have nearly $400 million from that relatively small amount. Amazing! Even at a less ambitious 12 percent compounded, $25,000 would turn into a healthy bounty of more than $3 million.

The effects of compounding are dramatic, even mind-boggling, provided you can successfully implement a plan of action to bring about this wonderful result.

That, in a primitive way, was what I divined in the poolroom. Doubling my bet sounded easy. But in the case of my Dodgers bets, compounding after only three days became enormous bucks. It provided an excellent lesson, not only for the conduct of my life, but also for what it taught me about the stock market.

Hero Wanted

World War II was raging when I turned sixteen. I ran away from home and tried joining the army, but they said I was too young. The merchant marines said I was too skinny—five feet ten inches and just one hundred and fourteen pounds.

I didn't give up. I ate bananas until my belly ached because I heard it was a good way of gaining weight. What I wanted to do was to be like Colin P. Kelly, the great American hero who crashed his airplane into a Japanese battleship at Pearl Harbor. I thought it was a great way to go—so patriotic—so heroic.

I never made it to the war, still too young and too skinny even when the war ended.

Instead, I sold aluminum pots and pans door to door on the Lower East Side of New York and in Harlem, usually to poor people who bought them not because I was a great salesman, but because the down payment was only a dollar. They never intended to pay another penny and usually disappeared. I quit.

My father then paid a top craftsman $300 to train me as a diamond cutter, hoping I would finally develop a trade at which I could earn a living. One night, as we put the diamonds back into the safe, two guys robbed the place. Scared out of my wits, I jumped out the window and ran down the fire escape. I never went back.

I wasn't any good at it, anyway. I once forgot about a diamond on the polishing machine and let it grind down to dust. My boss was frustrated and angry, to say the least. My ineptness made a mockery of the craft.

Jobs, Jobs, Jobs

I was like the young man in the story who kept going from one job to the next, unable to hold on to any of them. Finally, he got a position as a salesman in a fancy china store. The second day at work he accidentally smashed a large, expensive vase. He was called to the owner's office and entered nervously. The owner told him, "Young man, since you broke that expensive vase, its cost will be deducted from your wages every week until it is totally repaid in the sum of $15,000!" "Terrific!" the young man replied. "A steady job—at last!"

I worked in a fruit store where I spent half my time begging the customers not to squeeze the fruit and the other half being screamed at by my boss for allowing customers to squeeze the fruit.

As I got older, I took a little more initiative, trying at every opportunity to make a little money. I had one idea to make a killing on the holidays. On Mother's Day I was out at six A.M. selling silk scarves on a busy street corner. On Father's Day I was back on the same corner selling nickel handkerchiefs.

I did almost anything and everything. I picked up pins in a bowling alley and laid out shop windows for an interior designer. I worked nights in a bakery and, after catching only a few hours' sleep, I got up early to drive a taxi—a worthwhile job, since now I can maneuver my way through the heavy Wall Street traffic. For a number of years I worked at hotels in the Catskills as a bellhop, salad man, busboy, and waiter, in that order.

What I didn't realize then was that I was learning how to get comfortable with versatility and hardship through all these dead-end jobs. I was learning persistence through all my defeats.

Late one spring, I showed up at a placement agency in Monticello, a popular mountain resort about two hours north of New York City, trying to land a summer job as a busboy or, better still, as a waiter. I was worried. With hundreds of guys waiting around ahead of me, I figured I'd never get a job. Just then, a call came in about a job in a fruit store on the outskirts of town paying the magnificent sum of $100 a week. Wow! What a break!

At the store, I eagerly described my experience. The man said, "Okay, you're hired."

I said, "Great, wonderful. When do I start?"

"Right now," he answered.

"What are the hours?" I asked.

He glanced at me scornfully.

"You just lost the job," he said.

I was dumbfounded.

"What do you mean?" I wailed.

"Listen," he said. "We are a summer resort. We open July Fourth, we close Labor Day. We've got to make it all in those ten weeks! We work from now right through Labor Day, all day, all night, all summer. You sleep when you can, where you can—on the potato bags if you must."

That was the fastest I ever lost a job. Never again in my life did I ask about hours or other conditions. If I wanted a job, I said, "Okay, I'll take it."

This is a discipline I follow to this day. I don't ask about hours. I don't look a gift horse in the mouth. I just immerse myself in my job totally, completely dedicated to doing the very best at whatever I do.

Another summer I worked as a "special" waiter—a job that involved serving other waiters. One time I was impatient to get out and play like everybody else, so I washed off the plastic tablecloths carelessly. They fired me on the spot. It made a great impact—the pain of being fired, the mortifying embarrassment. I made up my mind then and there that I would never again be shamed like that. I would try to do every job, no matter how menial it may seem, to perfection.

Mʏ Cᴏᴍᴇʙᴀᴄᴋ

I was always on the lookout for a new opportunity to make money. I wanted, more than anything, to be a success.

My life could basically be summed up with the old adage "G-d helps those who help themselves." I really believed that somehow G-d would make me do better. Perhaps I lived in a dream world but

I always felt intuitively that one day I would succeed. Thankfully, G-d gave me the talent, the energy, and the determination to achieve, but until then, I let my virtues lie fallow.

I hadn't learned much in religious school because I rebelled early and paid little attention. But of everything they attempted to teach me, one value eventually got through. In Judaism, the highest form of serving G-d is studying and learning. Judaism taught that anything you learn has a value and can be a learning experience and a guide for living life. I always retained this respect for the value of education.

As a result, when I stopped rebelling, I went back to school at night. But the only night school in the neighborhood was an all-girls high school that became coed at night; that's why my high school diploma reads that I graduated from "Central Girls High."

After graduating from high school at age twenty, I entered Brooklyn College, taking night classes, part time, the minimum number of courses.

It took me eight years to graduate; by then, I was married with three children and I peddled vacuum cleaners during the day and worked in the Bethlehem shipyards on Staten Island at night after class.

The Long and Short of It

That's where I first sold a stock short. An untrained assistant, I did the most mundane chores. I carried tools to the ship and back and sandpapered rust, endlessly, off the deck and sides of the ship. I would be sent off ship to requisition tools and bring them back to the master tradesmen.

I'd be scared out of my wits because I had to climb up and down a rope ladder with one hand full of heavy tools. I'd never before realized how high those ships were, but they were more than seven stories high and to me it might have been the top of the Empire State Building. I have always been deathly afraid of heights.

And the time I wasted? Just to get a tool took me at least half an hour—leaving the ship, getting down the ladder, going to requisition the tools, waiting in line, coming back, and climbing up. Then it would take me four hours to sandpaper seven inches of rust.

"My G-d," I thought, "this company is so inefficient. They've got to lose money. It must be a great stock short!" And so I shorted Bethlehem Steel, the owner of Bethlehem Shipyards.

As I said, it was my first experience selling short. Selling short means that you sell what you don't own, hoping to buy it back at a lower price than you sold at, if and when it finally drops. Your profit is the difference between the sale price—the price at which you sold it—and the purchase price at which you buy it back.

I figured that when the rest of the United States discovered what I saw up close—the outlandish inefficiency of Bethlehem Steel—the stock would fall apart and I could buy it back much cheaper and make a killing. Unfortunately for me, it never happened.

As the stock moved up, I got margin calls every day. I put up more money, thinking that before long the world would discover the truth about Bethlehem's incompetence. Instead, the stock split 5 for 1 (in those days steel stocks were very hot) and I wound up completely wiped out. Instead of making a killing, I got killed.

What I salvaged from that debacle was the lesson that observing only part of a company is no way to invest. I failed to realize that the more time I spent on my tasks and the more time the other employees and I wasted, the more the company made. Bethlehem Steel charged the government "cost plus," and they make big money on that no-lose formula. My work was being billed at perhaps $25 an hour while I was paid about 50 cents.

What I, with my limited viewpoint, saw as waste and inefficiency, brought record earnings to Bethlehem Shipyards. In fact, earnings exploded. They knew how to bill out my work.

I learned plenty about the stock market that way. You must study a company, analyze its situation and the source of its earnings before you invest. It's easy to make assumptions where, in fact, the opposite is true. Don't make important financial decisions based on piecemeal, fragmentary, and ill-investigated information.

A VACUUM IN MY LIFE

My first experience as an Electrolux vacuum cleaner door-to-door salesman was a disaster. My wife, Rozi, and I had never been on Staten Island before. We had always lived in Brooklyn, which had apartment houses or multiple-family brownstones with lobbies or hallways or vestibules you would walk into to ring the bell. We had never been to a one-family home in our lives. Rozi sat in the car encouraging me as I embarked on my new career as a vacuum cleaner salesman. I knocked on the door of the first house we stopped at and walked right in—to what I figured was the lobby or vestibule.

But when I walked through that door, I suddenly found myself in the middle of the housewife's living room. When she saw me, she started screaming and threatening to call the cops. I finally calmed her down and convinced her to allow me to do a demonstration. She insisted I do it quickly, before her dinner guests arrived. I confidently poured dirt all over her carpet knowing my handy-dandy Electrolux vacuum cleaner would do the job. How was I to know the woman's electricity was out of order? The enraged woman once again threatened to call the authorities. I grabbed my vacuum cleaner and ran.

Rozi persuaded me to try again, so I walked around the side of the house figuring it was a different apartment. How was I to know that it was a one-family house and that this was her side door? This time she really went crazy. This time she did call the police.

Being a door-to-door salesman taught me a lot about hard knocks and rejection and the great value of perseverance. Eventually, just through persistence and longer hours than anybody else, I sold more vacuum cleaners than any salesman in my territory.

I used to canvass door to door, which is a most unpleasant thing because ninety-nine out of one hundred people slam the door in your face.

One day, my father-in-law, a warm, determined super-salesman, told me, "One woman out of a hundred is waiting for you. Just persevere, keep knocking, and you'll find that one person." After that, every time someone slammed a door on me, I would say, "Now only ninety-eight more, now ninety-seven, now ninety-six," and so on.

Later, I entered the brokerage business and started working for Walter Sloan, one of the most successful producers on Wall Street, at Shields and Company. He said, "All I do all day is stay on the phone and keep calling and calling. Of one hundred calls, one guy calls me back or one guy in one hundred is actually waiting for my call.

"As you get successful, your success rate goes up and you succeed more often. Just stay on that phone. Keep making those calls. Most people don't want to do that because it hurts their egos to be hung up on, to be rejected. You have to learn how to overcome or accept that. It is part of the price. As you work at it and get better, as you make it and become really outstanding, then two or three out of one hundred will respond to you." It was a powerful lesson to learn and my desire to succeed at something I had once miserably failed at helped me a lot when I later went into sales again. But that would not be for a long while.

Still, all of the early aggravation was good preparation. It prepared me to deal with the tough life I would later cope with in the brokerage business. In fact, once I had an office with a desk and my own phone, it felt like a miracle to me just to be moderately comfortable. It was a pleasure not to have people slam the door on me, not to be snowed or rained upon, not to be sweating from the summer heat, not to be stuck with my broken-down, forsaken old jalopy. When people hung up on me or were rude on the telephone, I could say to myself, "So what? It's great compared to what I used to go through.'' Even the intermittent, sharp market drops over the ensuing years that gave us all sleepless nights and heartaches and ulcers seemed more bearable to me because I knew what else the hard world held.

THE WIFE IN MY LIFE

My life was far from an instant success story. It was actually a miracle that I found the right path. But it was not all of my doing. Others played a big part, mainly my father-in-law and my mother-in-law. But the single most important person, the one who gave my life focus and direction and meaning and motivation, was my wife, Rozi. When people talk about family values, this, to me is what they're talking about—how much your love for, and relationship with, members of your family can contribute to your character, your happiness, and your success in the world.

Rozi and I met at a beach in the Rockaways the summer I was eighteen. She was the sweetest, most serene beauty I had ever seen, blond and rosy-cheeked, with a pretty turned-up nose. In fact, she won a beauty contest—Miss Young Israel of New York. She was also warm and personable with wonderful basic values.

Every guy in the neighborhood was after her. Many summer nights when I came to take her out, one guy was eagerly waiting for her on the front porch and another was on the back porch. Meanwhile, she enticed me into washing the dishes in the kitchen for her mother and cut out with one of the other guys. I washed a lot of dishes before I finally won her, but it was a good lesson in tenacity.

If I ever did manage to get a night out with Rozi, I used my father's old station wagon reeking of salami from his daily deliveries— he sold salamis, bolognas, hot dogs, corned beef, pastrami, etc., out of the back of his ''truck''—and she always ''schlepped'' along a few girlfriends for the ride. Still, I was madly in love. I chased her until

I wore her down and she finally accepted me. My wife says I knew how to pick a winner even then.

ALL WE HAD WAS LOVE

The only apartment we could afford originally was half of one big apartment which had been divided into two. It was only one room that you entered by walking through the bathroom.

What a dump. Before we ate meals, Rozi and I spent a few minutes stomping on the floor, scaring away all the mice. But at least it was a roof over our heads. However, that turned out to be too expensive for us, so we moved in with my in-laws. We lived in Rozi's old bedroom until our second baby was born.

Rozi and I were in college together. During the eight years I was in school, we had three of our four daughters. For our first baby's delivery, Rozi and I went to a doctor where we paid one dollar for each visit. For our next two daughters' deliveries Rozi switched to a clinic because it charged only a quarter a visit.

It took me eight years to graduate because I attended classes mainly at night. I needed to hold two or three part-time jobs so that we could afford to live. At this time we were living on Staten Island—a long ferry ride from school and jobs.

Blessedly, Rozi and the kids were very understanding of my long hours of studying. Once Rozi went out to substitute in a local school. I was hard at my studies with only one ear listening for my kids busily playing in the other room. After three hours, Rozi returned and found the whole apartment flooded with bubbles. It was like an episode of *I Love Lucy*. The kids were all sitting on top of the washing machine, which overflowed and poured forth pools of soapsuds. After laying out every towel we owned and could borrow, Rozi asked the kids why they hadn't called me—after all, I was in the next room. They answered, "Mommy, you told us not to bother Daddy when he's studying."

Those years at Brooklyn College were hard because I worked all day and studied all night. I had aching shoulders and a strained back from dragging bundles in my door-to-door days and itching, burning eyes from studying at night combined with terrible allergies.

In June 1957, I graduated from Brooklyn College. I was twenty-eight years old.

Commencement ceremonies were held on the Sunday of the Memorial Day weekend. I was graduating magna cum laude, Phi Beta Kappa, and receiving the Economics Award. All of my friends and relatives planned to attend such a major event.

My story—graduating, at the top of my class, Phi Beta Kappa, after so many difficult years and so many different jobs with a wife and family to support—seemed newsworthy from a human interest point of view, because Brooklyn College sent out press releases and the *Staten Island Advance* newspaper took pictures of me and my wife and our three daughters. The New York *Herald Tribune,* the *Journal American,* the *World Telegram,* and the *Daily Mirror* also ran stories, as did the *Daily News.* Even the prestigious *New York Times* ran a little blurb.

Unfortunately, I was already working my summer job as a waiter in the Catskills. The Memorial Day weekend was a big moneymaker at the resorts and I drove upstate to the Pioneer Country Club to wait tables since we were in urgent need of the cash. I hurriedly served my tables, planning to race back to Brooklyn in time for graduation exercises. But I had to wait around until late Sunday afternoon for my tips.

I raced like a wild man to get back to Brooklyn College only to get stuck in terrible Sunday traffic. When I finally arrived, the auditorium was empty—except for my relatives and the janitors who were folding chairs. Between the aggravation of waiting around so long for tips and the bumper-to-bumper traffic, I missed the graduation completely. All I could do was pose for a few pictures in my cap and gown with my wife and little girls on the empty dais. Then we all turned around and went back to my job in the mountains.

HOT TIPS BURN

During the years when we really stretched our dollars, Rozi and I learned a lesson we will never forget.

We attended a small birthday party for a child of a friend of ours that turned out to be the most expensive affair we would ever attend. Since we were very poor, we really agonized over how much to spend on a gift. Should it be $3 or $4?

At the party, our friend, a stockbroker, told us about a spectacular land exploration company in the Southwest—the New Mexico & Arizona Land Company. Though we could hardly afford it, we took the very last of our savings and bought 100 shares at $18 on margin.

For the next few months, this broker friend called us up every single day, telling us of the most wondrous developments. The company discovered gold, silver, and much more. Yet somehow, with each new find, the stock went down, even though our broker kept assuring us that it would be great. The stock dropped to half and then *less* than half. Meanwhile, we kept getting margin calls. When I finally had no more money, we received a last call telling us that we were sold out, wiped out! We lost all our money at the most disastrous time. I was borrowing money in order to live and it was the only principal I had.

Had we been smart, we would have given the kid $1,800 as a birthday present. Our friend would have been elated and we would have looked like two of the nicest, most generous people in the whole world. That's what the party cost us: $1,800 plus the $4 we spent for the actual gift, our life savings at the time!

With that experience, I learned how some brokers can operate. I learned that creative new rumors can hypnotize people into hanging on to their stock and how shallow the information can be on which supposedly sophisticated brokers make their "sure thing" recommendations.

Because of this, I always warned clients to disregard get-rich-quick tips they picked up in clubs or at social events. If you feel that your source is knowledgeable and that the idea has merit, then look into it yourself, I argued. Learn all about the company. Check it out with someone who is an expert in the area or who has made a lot of money investing wisely.

I learned the hard way that winning the competitive battle of Wall Street requires being alert every minute of every day. Don't rely, as I did, on limited information or on some "hot-tip" broker. You must not only be up psychologically, but also up on all the information that is available on your objectives. Remember that knowledge is power. And stupidity is expensive.

OPPORTUNITY KNOCKS

Discouraged with my employment opportunities, right after we married, Rozi and I decided to go into business for ourselves—a lucrative business—umbrellas. It was during the Korean War and there was a shortage of steel. We collected rusty, broken, steel umbrella frames off the streets and out of junkyards, tore off the original material, bent the frames back into shape, and dipped them into silver aluminum paint. We negotiated a deal with an umbrella company to sell them five hundred frames. We worked out of an old garage and even hired a young kid to work for us. One night, when we already had more than four hundred umbrellas, the kid left a cigarette burning. The flammable silver paint exploded, taking our umbrellas, our garage, and our dreams up in smoke.

Then, evolving out of my career selling vacuum cleaners and other general merchandise came the opportunity of a lifetime. I was offered a partnership in my father-in-law's door-to-door sales business selling linen, pots, tablecloths, oversized coats, and an "exclusive" line of nickel handkerchiefs.

I was tempted by this offer, which at the time seemed like a secure, if limited, future. But my aspirations had changed—my goals had now been set higher. I had become aware of the Harvard Business School and of the opportunities a Harvard education could offer me.

I took a big risk by going to Harvard with a young wife, three little children, and no money, but it turned out to be one of the best decisions I ever made. Harvard transformed my life.

FROM INSECURITIES TO SECURITIES

At that time, the average Harvard Business School graduate, ten years out, made $25,000 a year. It was stupendous. In the mid-1950s, that was like saying that the average Harvard Business School graduate ten years out was making $500,000 a year in today's dollars.

On my first day at Harvard, I looked around and saw ninety guys in my section. The well-publicized statistics were that 10 percent of the students in every entering class flunked out. "My G-d," I said to myself, "these classmates of mine are all geniuses!" Some of them had British accents or fine southern drawls. I was impressed. I thought they were all so articulate that I was absolutely bound to be the one who would fail. As it turned out, I graduated at the top of my class with highest honors. So why was I so fearful?

It was in the nature of my upbringing to be insecure.

At least two factors were involved. One was cultural. Being Jewish often made me feel that I had to constantly prove myself by working three times as hard as anyone else. Even though I knew that many Jewish students excelled at Harvard, I, for one, didn't feel that I belonged and always felt compelled to prove my intelligence. I think many of my classmates who weren't Jewish were secure enough to feel that just by being accepted at Harvard, they belonged. Fortunately, I do believe that much of this has changed since I attended Harvard.

Another factor that contributed to my lack of self-confidence was my father. A decent and charitable man who always gave beyond his means, he worked hard but never succeeded.

His own brothers treated him with contempt. They excluded him from a profitable family meat business, hiring him only as a self-employed delivery man. Since my father was the least successful of his brothers, they constantly belittled him. One of his brothers, though childless, acted as if he knew better than anyone how to raise children and would always tell my father that he was raising us all wrong.

They never treated my father with any measure of respect. At family gatherings, his brothers were treated royally, while my father was stuck at a remote table as an irrelevant afterthought. It was so embarrassing. It may be that my father's painful humiliation underlies my own drive for success. I saw what my father was and how he suffered and I suffered with him.

Sadly, my father's frustration and bitterness made him short-tempered and critical of me. He constantly put me down, telling me I would never amount to anything.

"You're a nothing and you'll always be a nothing!" he yelled.

So, while I was virtually at the head of my class at business school, I still always felt as if failure was imminent.

My need to succeed, implanted so early, grew out of the Depression years as well. People then dreaded loss and had a fear of devastating poverty, of winding up completely broke and in a poorhouse in their old age. They don't feel that today. Most people are no longer so strongly motivated by insecurity and the need to overcome it, so they lack this same drive to succeed.

Everyone during the Depression felt an intense hunger and drive. I knew that unless I worked hard I would have nothing. An internal whip still drives me. Nobody forces me to sit down Saturday night and Sunday to work. It's certainly not for the money anymore. Yet, I will frequently stay up until three o'clock in the morning, until I am totally exhausted, reading, analyzing my accounts, or studying stocks.

*   *   *

The Harvard experience is unique in its intense pressure, the fight first to survive and then to excel.

For two years I studied with unrelenting determination. Fortunately, I went to business school with some actual business experience. It made my education far more valuable to me than to the young kids right out of college. I learned how to learn, study, and adapt. I learned how different the case method was from the perspectives I was taught, because there was no right or wrong answer. You could get an A or an F for the same answer. And someone diametrically opposed to your position could get the same grade. It depended on how you documented your answer, the facts you used, as well as your aspirations and hopes. The decision wasn't as important as the rationale behind it.

Before exams many of the guys would take No-Doz in order to have precious extra hours to study. They stayed up studying for exams right through the night. One fellow who did this came to the exam after several sleepless nights and was so tired he filled up five pages in his blue book just writing his name over and over. Another guy entered the classroom alert and ready, but as soon as the professor handed him the test paper, he laid down his head and slept, unwakeable, right through the test.

I remember a night after my very first exam when Rozi and I thought that all my hopes and dreams were down the toilet. My professor said that as soon as he graded each paper he would post the mark in Aldrich Hall so we need not wait until the next day for our first results of the term. An unmarried friend living on campus promised to call me as soon as my grade came down. Rozi and I were nervous wrecks and I couldn't concentrate on my studying. I was one of the first called. My grade? D. We were completely devastated. We didn't answer the phone for the rest of the evening so that we wouldn't have to divulge our humiliation to anyone. We stayed up all through the night making alternate plans for our life.

At nine-thirty the next morning I found out that there had been eighteen Us—unsatisfactory; twenty LPs—low pass; twenty-seven Ps—pass; twenty-two HPs—high pass; and only three Ds out of a class of ninety students. Miraculously, D stood for Distinction. It was the highest grade you could get at the Harvard Business School.

WHACKED OUT

I wanted to really be a part of the Harvard spirit. So, at five feet ten inches and weighing in at one hundred and twenty-five pounds, I went out for the intramural football team, joining teammates who were at least six feet two and weighed close to two hundred pounds.

I came running to our first practice a little late, waving to the guys, screaming "I'm coming" as if they were just waiting for me, their star player. In my rush I tripped over the low wire protecting the grass, fell on my face unconscious, and had to be taken off the field and home on a stretcher. I never even got into the game, but my wife and kids were proud that I was a football casualty hero.

During my first game, the other team was close to their goal line. I had a great plan of attack. I decided to plunge head on with all my might into a big hulk of a guy. When the play started, I got set and threw my body totally at him. He just stepped aside and I fell, embarrassingly, flat on my face.

That was my first and last game.

OF TICKER TAPES AND TABLECLOTHS

If there was anything I wanted from Harvard, it was an escape from selling, which I hated.

So I went into research.

Between your first and second year at Harvard, you're advised to take a summer job, so I interned as a research analyst at Loeb Rhoades, an old, established Wall Street firm. In situations like that, if the company likes you, it hires you back after you graduate. The summer job is a learning opportunity—about yourself and what you might do after college. You're introduced to a company and the company is introduced to you.

While working at Loeb Rhoades that summer, I heard a rumor from a well-informed friend of mine that a particular company was going to be taken over. It sounded good! It was getting late on a summer Friday afternoon and I couldn't find the head of my department, so I barged up to the executive office to see John Loeb, the senior partner himself. I was just a summer employee, one of hundreds, and a little summer employee just didn't just go in to see John Loeb—the chairman of the board. But, naïvely, I did. And I told him what I'd heard.

On Monday morning a memo was circulated throughout the organization telling us all about the lines of communication, the table of organization of the company, and who could talk to whom—all because I, a mere summer employee, dared pay that visit to the chairman's office.

I was ambitious and eager to be noticed. I wanted to do great things and I worked hard at research. Each Monday morning, I wrote summaries of all the various investment services' reports, including those of Standard & Poor, Value Line, and so on. During the rest of the week, I answered inquiries about stocks for members of our correspondent group. We cleared for many other brokerage firms, including requests such as "What do you think of American Telephone?" I did the research for our responses.

Our director of research at Loeb Rhoades was Dr. Eric Rinner, a very strict, pedantic German academician. He called me "Davidowitz." That's my name to this day. I only use "Davis" because when I first entered the brokerage business and said I was Morty Davidowitz, people would say "What? How do you spell it? How do you pronounce it?" Just to cut out all the lengthy clarification, I used "Davis," but I never changed my name legally.

At summer's end, Dr. Rinner called me in for an interview. "Davidowitz," he said, "I want to tell you something. You are a very bright guy, but you don't belong here in research."

"Why not?" I asked in dismay.

"You don't have the ass for it," he said.

I couldn't believe my ears. "What do you mean?" I asked.

"To do research," he explained, "you must sit down on your ass and sit there consistently, hour after hour, all day, reading and digging and analyzing and doing spreadsheets."

I was crushed. And yet it was one of the biggest favors anyone ever did for me. Sometimes put-downs that seem the most devastating thing at the time are really good lessons. They tell you what you shouldn't be doing, what you can't do. Dr. Rinner did me a great service because he was right. That summer job at Loeb Rhoades made me realize that whatever job I ultimately took, I desperately needed the action, the dynamism, that just being a sedate, passive research analyst could never, ever provide. I needed to be at the center of things where I could be constantly active and decisive.

For us to survive during my second year at Harvard, Rozi worked for a man in the catering business. Every week he dropped off the tablecloths from that week's affairs and Rozi spent her nights sewing up the cigarette burns. She received 10 cents per hole. Late into the night, after the kids were asleep, I'd study and she'd sew. The two of us prayed that lots of people would carelessly smoke; we needed those burn holes. We desperately needed the money.

Unfortunately, with this as our major source of income, and despite the fact that I was graduating at the top of my class and dying to attend the ceremony, we could not stay in Boston for the graduation. There was no way we could afford even one more week's rent. We packed up our few belongings and headed for New York.

REAL RICHES

My in-laws owned a three-family house in the Boro Park section of Brooklyn and after my graduation from Harvard, we lived there rent free.

Rozi comes from a warm, stable family. She and her brothers and parents loved religion, which to me, as a child, represented only prohibitions, restrictions, and deprivations—taboos I couldn't understand and therefore resented. But after I married Rozi, the love she and her family felt for religion had a very positive effect on me.

My father-in-law was a unique person. He was a warm and caring man who gave abundantly of his wisdom, his time, and his wonderful insights, not only from the teachings of the biblical sages, but from his own extensive travels and experiences.

I was my mother-in-law's greatest admirer. I learned from her strength, her optimism, and her true appreciation of life. She always said I was her favorite son-in-law. Of course, being her only son-in-law, I didn't have much competition. Both Rozi's parents made me feel like a real son. They considered a close-knit family to be an essential ingredient to a fulfilling life.

My wife and I and our kids lived in the attic apartment of their three-story house while my brother-in-law Irving and his family lived next door. For years, another brother-in-law, Morris, and his five children lived with my in-laws in their cramped first-floor apartment.

One day my father-in-law came running breathlessly up the stairs to speak to me. "Morris wants to take his family and move away, out of our apartment," he cried frantically. "Why do they need to move? We have plenty of room in our apartment for them. Please, Morty, talk some sense into him. Mama is upset."

I calmed my father-in-law down, agreeing to speak to Morris.

"Where does Morris want to move?" I asked.

"Away! One flight up—to the second-floor apartment," he answered.

Now, some thirty years later, my daughters and their families have all settled very close to our home, and I suppose that if any of them moved too far away, I too would ask that someone talk some sense into them.

Though it was overcrowded and cramped in those early years and though I didn't take to it instantly, that close family pattern turned out to be one of the truly greatest blessings of my life.

Old Values, New Issues

An appreciation for religion became another blessing. I think there are three basic foundations to religion: the theological, the social, and the moral. The one that came to mean the most to me is the social—the roots, the tradition, and the warmth.

I learned to enjoy and appreciate the Sabbath because it is so truly and completely a day of rest. It is unparalleled in its pleasantness and serenity. We spend time with family on the Sabbath. We eat, talk, sing, and even make love, which, incidentally, is considered a "mitzvah," or a good deed, because by indulging in the reproductive endeavor we are following the Biblical precept "Be fruitful, and multiply."

The Sabbath is an uplifting day, intellectually and spiritually. I almost never miss a Friday dinner or a Saturday noon meal with my family. What once struck me as restrictions, I now see as liberation. Our Sabbath is unique. We can't make or take telephone calls, we can't turn on the TV or drive or do business of any kind. This forces a different kind of day on me. I converse, I study, I interact. The family gets to know and enjoy each other. We grow by sharing the warmth of family and friends.

From the outside, you may say, "That's backward," and in a way it is. But it has a very useful function. It is the one true day of rest. That framework forces you to be more related—more human, in effect.

After an especially intense week of work, it is a much appreciated time of regeneration of the body and the mind. I feel renewed, excited, and uplifted. As it turns out, it is not a day of deprivation, as I once thought, but a day of revitalization, of love and warmth and of stopping to appreciate the worth of friends, children, family, life, health, nature—the nonmaterialistic, truly worthwhile things that make our world potentially so wonderful.

I came a long way in life, but my family and my religion are truly my greatest riches.

End of Chpt. 8

CHAPTER NINE

THE BEGINNING OF SOMETHING BIG

When I graduated from Harvard in 1959, I sent out hundreds of résumés in all directions. I knew I wanted to go to Wall Street, but beyond that I hadn't really found myself.

I wasn't overwhelmed with offers. Perhaps, despite my Harvard degree and excellent academic credentials, I was still too much the Brooklyn boy without the requisite polish. Some friends suggested that it was because my résumé said "Davidowitz," rather than "Cabot" or "Lodge"—coincidentally, the actual names of two of my bright fellow classmates. I'll never know whether that theory had any merit—in any case, I was who I was.

Two incidents showed me that no matter how much education you have there is still no substitute for a little experience. On one of my first interviews, I was invited to lunch with a partner of the firm. I was excited and eager to make a positive impression. Because I had never gone on a business lunch before, I didn't know what was proper to order. After some consideration, I decided on a tuna fish sandwich because I felt it was safe. I was very nervous and was trying to act sophisticated and at ease. When my sandwich arrived, in an effort to display proper etiquette, I began eating it with a knife and fork. The partner smiled and said, "It's okay to pick it up."

Another time when I was starting out in the brokerage business, my wife came up to the office and did some secretarial work for me. I was sitting at my desk when I received a phone call from a woman. She said she wanted to invest a huge sum of money. I was ecstatic.

She gave me specific instructions on how and where she wanted her money invested. Before hanging up, she said, "Do me a favor and look to your left." I did. There was my wife waving to me and throwing me kisses. She was my new client.

I realized that success doesn't come that easily or that quickly. "Some day," Rozi said, "when we really have the money, you will be my broker and other people will invest lots of money with you."

The beginning was hard, but at least we kept our sense of humor.

I'M ON MY WAY

My first job was not exactly right for me. I was offered a position by Mr. Donald Arthur, the head of Shields & Company. He'd formerly been a partner of Price Waterhouse, the major accounting firm, and was now a managing partner at Shields.

"We're doing a lot of business with Jewish corporate clients," he told me. "At Shields we've never had a Jewish partner and we'd like to have one. With your background at the Harvard Business School, you can be an asset to us. You're articulate and attractive. We'd like you to come into management and ultimately be our first Jewish partner."

Having been rejected by so many other firms, I was grateful to be appreciated and especially to be offered an eventual partnership at Shields—I grabbed the job.

I was in management no more than four or five months when I realized it was not right for me. All the guys around me, all the salesmen and brokers, were making big money and I took care of the headaches. People came to me when there was a problem with an account, when there was a margin call, or when there was a regulatory compliance question.

I swallowed my pride. It took a lot of guts. Although I went to Harvard to get out of selling, I told my bosses that, despite my degree and my management title, I wanted to become a salesman, a stock-broker. And I did.

I loved it from the start.

I didn't ask anybody how much I would earn. I stayed on the phone as long as I wanted and when I made a sale and wrote a trade ticket, it was a commission paid right then and there. Everybody else went home but I stayed until the very last minute. I continued calling, even after eleven o'clock at night, until people said, "You have a hell of a lot of nerve calling at this hour." Finally, reluctantly, I'd leave because I realized that from then on any further calls would be counterproductive.

I didn't stop at lunchtime, when all the other brokers visited and shot the bull. They thought I was antisocial, but it wasn't that. They were nice enough guys. I just wanted so much to make it.

They were years ahead of me and I wanted to catch up.

As it happened, the harder I worked, the more productive I became. It was like compounding. Working twice as hard, I caught up ten times as fast as each account led to recommendations and more new accounts.

It was very much like that penny on a checkerboard. Start with one cent, double it on each square of the board sixty-four times, and you end up with more than a quadrillion pennies—more than all the money in the United States. If you start with only a single dollar after only twenty doubles, you're past a million dollars. Analogously, when you double your efforts every day and every week, that is no mere double in a year. For me it turned out to be a double every two months.

So, with my idea of working neurotically hard, I more than caught up. In my first full year of working as a broker, I was the second-highest producer in our entire organization—second among the vast number of brokers at Shields.

MY FIRST BIG ACCOUNT

My first major client was an eighty-year-old man, Carl Siroty, whom I met by chance at a restaurant. Siroty was seated at the next table. My childhood friend Stuart Slater, a pharmacist I was having dinner with, boisterously started up a conversation with this total stranger and before long introduced me, because I was certainly still too shy to just up and talk to a stranger in a restaurant. Suddenly, Siroty pulled out of his breast pocket a bunch of lined sheets, his portfolio. It was unbelievable. He owned every big security on the market—$3 million in AT&T, $7 million in McDonnell Douglas, $5 million in Martin Marietta. His portfolio was worth about $40 million in 1959 dollars. The equivalent today would be several hundred million dollars. It was just an enormous account.

I was dying for his account, so I kept in constant, persistent touch with him. I practically moved in with him and every so often he'd give me a little business. He was the type who fought with everyone, and when he inevitably had a falling out with his main broker, the account became mine.

He was a multimillionaire, but as miserly and, sadly, as ornery as they come. I'd meet him for dinner to discuss his investments and invariably he said, "Order the goulash, it's very good." Not to mention that it was the cheapest item on the menu. He ordered steak, saying that his doctor told him he needed iron. I, of course, ordered the goulash.

His hotel apartment was about sixty blocks (more than three miles) from the restaurant where we used to eat. After dinner he pulled the same shtick. I'd say, "Let's get a cab," and he'd say, "Let's walk a little." Then, after about twenty blocks, he'd say, "You know what? We're almost there. It doesn't pay to take a cab. Let's walk the rest of the way." He was so cheap; he just wouldn't spring for the cab. He knew if we took the cab he should pay for it or it would look bad. After all, he was a multimillionaire and I was just starting out.

He wanted every minute of my time, especially when Rozi and the kids were up in the Catskill mountains for the summer. He insisted I stay in the city and be available early. He offered a room for me at his hotel—the Paris Hotel on West End Avenue at Ninety-second Street and a seedy second-class one at that. Then, when we arrived at the hotel, even though I saw the hotel manager standing at the desk, he told me, "It seems no one's on duty." "Okay," he'd say, "you can sleep on the couch in my apartment." He was too tight to pay for a room for me.

He had me on call twenty-four hours a day. He demanded attention and I gave it to him because I badly wanted the business an account that immense generated.

He really wasn't a very nice guy. One time I hired an assistant, Peter, on Siroty's urging, because Peter's mother was a friend of his. Siroty called and Peter picked up the phone. Siroty gave him an order to buy 20,000 shares of Lear Siegler. Peter called him back and said that he had executed the trade at 37.

"Thirty-seven!" Siroty yelled. "I wanted it at 35½."

"But," insisted Peter, "you only told me to buy! 'Hurry up and buy it,' you said! You didn't specify at what price you would take it. You didn't give me a price limit!"

"I won't take it at 37!" Siroty yelled. "It's yours!"

My assistant was devastated. He was a young kid. Where could he get the money to cover the trade? Including commissions it was well over $740,000. For almost two weeks I tried convincing Siroty to take the stock, but he wouldn't hear of it. He hung up on me. He wouldn't see me. He wouldn't even talk to Peter or me or, for that matter, anyone at the firm who tried calling him and urging him to pay for the purchase of the Lear Siegler shares he had ordered.

Then one day the stock had a run-up to $39. I called Siroty. He answered the call and I said, "Peter thanks you for letting him buy the 20,000 shares of Lear Siegler at $37 a share. It's terrific. He's making so much money. He's elated." Siroty yelled, "What, are you crazy? What are you talking about, what do you mean his stock? It's my stock! If he wants shares, let him go buy his own! There's plenty of stock on the market!''

This one account occupied almost all of my time. I couldn't move from my desk because Siroty got angry if I wasn't there, answering his calls. I was doing well, but I couldn't grow very much spending so much of my time servicing this one account, lucrative as it might be. So after much thought and plenty of sleepless nights, I resigned the account I so desperately pursued and worked so hard to acquire. Siroty was furious. It was a most trying move for me, but it left me with time to expand my horizons—to get into investment banking and venture capital.

Wall Street is a small place—even though people on the outside think of it as a vast world in itself, if you are good, others hear about it. Very quickly, I was noticed and got offers from other firms. In December 1961, only two years after I joined Shields, I was offered a partnership with D.H. Blair. I was flattered, and accepted.

It was a small company, but to be offered a partnership, even a nominal partnership, in those days was a real accomplishment, especially for me. Remember, I hadn't even been able to get a job on Wall Street, try as I might, before I went to Harvard. Now I was becoming a partner, which seemed to me to be the greatest achievement in the world.

MAKING IT

D.H. Blair was a small, unimportant firm when I joined it in 1961. Over the years, I changed its direction and stature dramatically. Today, we are number one in the particular niche we occupy: funding young growth companies.

Years and years of hard work produced gratifying success. It's just like a drop of water on a rock. Each drop is infinitesimal in the effect it could possibly produce, while the rock seems impregnable. But after continuing years of persistence, the cumulative effect of the drops of water finally makes a significant dent and a deep impression.

I started out as a nominal partner with just a one percent partnership interest. By 1965, after only four years with Blair, I was bringing in more than half the profits of the firm, as well as inspiring over 70 percent of its projects and activities. Eventually I was rewarded with a 17 percent interest in the partnership.

When I joined Blair, the management of the firm was made up of eighteen general and eighteen limited partners. One day one of the older partners, Seymour Shorser, came up to me and said, "Someday, you're going to be the head of this whole operation. You're going to do big things." I was flabbergasted!

Since early on, I had always been told that I was never going to be any good, so I never really believed Shorser. I thought he was just flattering me. He was the first person who ever suggested that I might be that successful—the first to plant that seed in my mind.

As my production increased and I was bringing in about 70 or 80 percent of the firm's income, I felt exploited. I did all the work for only 17 percent of the company, while all the other partners ever did was hold meetings and talk about distributing the profits. On top of that, I was under severe pressure because of the nature of the job. I developed an ulcer. Ulcers, I'd heard, were at least partly psychosomatic, so I visited a psychologist for counseling.

He was a very wise man. Dr. Moses said, "You've got two options. Either slow down and do very little or work as hard as you always do. Slowing down will be counterproductive; it will only make you equal to the others. You'll bring in the same low percent of income that others do and you'll be average. You'll develop bad work habits. You'll lose the ability to be productive. You'll only hurt yourself. Your other alternative, continue to bring in your 80 percent of the profits regardless of the fact that your rewards may be lower than they should be—this may be the most valuable thing you can do right now.

"Build up your own accounts, your own reputation, your own

reservoir of intelligence," he advised. "It will pay off. In the short run you may lose something. You may be earning less than you deserve. But in the long run, Wall Street is a small place. Either somebody else will make you a proposition because they'll have learned about your talents and achievements, or your partners will ultimately make rewards commensurate with your production."

I took the doctor's advice. It was hard to swallow, but it was intelligent counsel, because ultimately I did end up with 100 percent of the company. Not because it was voluntarily awarded to me, but because the sequence of events brought me closer to 100 percent of my potential.

TO THE TOP

In 1969, the brokerage industry was in desperate trouble. Many firms went out of business, and there was a huge paper mess on Wall Street. Large amounts of money were lost within firms. Vast numbers of stocks disappeared because bookkeeping systems were too inefficient or ineffective to keep up with the volume. It's hard to believe but at 10 or 15 million shares a day—compared to today's average of several hundred million a day—we closed for half a day on Wednesdays and shortened trading hours because we couldn't otherwise handle the paperwork.

Many of the firms that went under had great names. When I was younger I would have given my eyeteeth to work with any of them at any job, not to mention attaining an esteemed partnership. They were the elite and no little Jewish boy from Brooklyn could ever think about a partnership with them. Yet here they were, going out of business—impressive, old-line firms such as F. I. du Pont & Co.; J. R. Williston & Beane Inc.; Goodbody & Company; Walston & Company; Hayden, Stone, Inc.; and a host of others, equally impressive and too numerous to list here. They disappeared or were absorbed into other firms.

At D.H. Blair, we had two or three losing months and the major partners got very nervous—scared out of their wits, in fact. In retrospect, they never really had the "in the trenches" training or ability requisite to make the firm work. They never really learned the business. One senior partner came out of the shoe business and inherited wealth. Another had a wealthy father who bought him a seat on the New York Stock Exchange.

Both were nice guys, but they didn't really know how to generate large income. So they invited younger people to become partners, desperately needing the income we produced.

Two brothers who owned the major part of the firm, inheritors of the wealth of the I. Miller & Sons shoe chain, had a terrible dispute and one of them left. The remaining senior partners feared that the departing brother might take most of the company with him—especially the younger stockbrokers who made up almost half of our producing individuals. So, to avoid this, and primarily out of fear of losing them rather than because they had earned it, they promoted en masse all of these young high-earning salesmen—who in most cases were not very brilliant businessmen—to the status of partners.

It's true that the young partners were productive salesmen, but in terms of building a solid business, they were not so productive that they all deserved partnerships. In most cases, they were just the beneficiaries of the senior partners' overwhelming fears in that critical moment.

It was an unhealthy move. When hard times came, management was cumbersome and lacked real leadership. The senior partners panicked. Having inherited their wealth, they didn't know how to make it back again if ever it was lost. Their real desire was simply to preserve their wealth.

"We should liquidate," they said. "We should close up."

"We haven't even begun to fight," I protested. "It's been only three or four bad months."

They were too frightened. "All of Wall Street is going down the drain. We'll be wiped out," they protested.

So I said, "Let me work at it. It's much too early to give up. Just give me an option. Let me try to turn the company around in six to nine months. I'll work much harder and get it straightened out. I'll make sure that we don't have losses. I'll make it a winning operation."

They finally succumbed and decided that the wisest thing to do was to give me an option on their shares. Each agreed to be reduced down to about one percent, retaining some position in the company. We put that in writing.

And I did turn it around. But when push came to shove, they balked. They wanted to reverse their position and rescind their agreement. They didn't want to let me exercise the option they'd extended. We held a meeting of all of the partners. They called for a vote. It was very embarrassing because one of the senior partners, someone I had considered my friend as well as my partner, accused me of wanting to take over the firm and urged the partners to vote against what they described as my "takeover."

I explained to all of the partners that that was my deal with them—and that it was on that basis that I worked my butt off day and night and weekends over many months. They made an agreement and I expected them to live up to it. I couldn't live with partners who were not true to their word.

And there was more. Expecting a confrontation, I purchased a seat on the New York Stock Exchange myself. At the end of this meeting—for me, a life-defining meeting—I said to the partners, "If you vote with the two senior partners who recommend that you not let me take over the overwhelming majority interest in D.H. Blair, I will leave and set up my own firm."

It was a long meeting, but when they finally took a vote, except for the two senior partners they voted unanimously in my favor. The senior partners turned over their shares to me. They had no choice.

And that is how, at age thirty-eight, only eight years after taking my first job on Wall Street just out of Harvard, I became the President and majority owner of D.H. Blair.

End of chpt. 9

III

WINNING WAYS ON WALL STREET

114.

Cht **TEN** $\rangle$ *gres to pg. 118... = 4 pgs*

THE STOCK MARKET CAN BE VOLATILE

A WORD OF WARNING

If you know that you lack the vision or emotional capacity for risk, don't try the stock market. My advice: Let others manage your money. Your results will be average, but involvement in anything as hard as this requires a tremendous personal investment. People like me spend every day and night of our lives using all of our energy and brains in this tough game.

And don't get involved part time and just throw your money in, either. Your results won't be average, you won't even do as well as a mutual fund. You will get killed.

That is my best entry-level advice. The market is not a game or a pastime. It's a profession and an opportunistic industry. And, although it offers immense rewards, if you can't afford to play the market financially or are not prepared for the emotional commitment and cost, stay out of the game and out of the market.

But if you think you have the potential for success—and many people really do but underestimate themselves—you will short-change yourself if you don't go for it. My advice to you is: Take a part of your funds and accept the big risks required. Recognize that you are taking a risk and go for the top of the world!

Remember, even if you don't make it, at least you tried. So few people really enjoy or exploit the adventure that life offers. If you go for the very top of the mountain and only get halfway there, you will still outstrip most of the rest of mankind. If you can, do it! It's an exciting, rewarding, fascinating experience.

This part of the book describes how you can make thousands or even millions in the market, either by choosing a winning stock and pyramiding your way to wealth or by starting your own winning company in a new area and taking it public. And finally, if you lack the time and energy to acquire this knowledge, this section will help you choose a superior broker whose advice and guidance can point you down Success Road.

I will tell you what I learned as an investor over the years. I will guide you through a life plan, what principles to adopt in choosing a winning stock, how to cut your losses, and how to choose a competent professional. I will provide a risk assumption formula, so that you can limit your exposure while you engage in the pursuit of significant wealth.

More than anything else, this section conveys the ideas and principles that produced success in the market for me.

Remember, you need only one great idea to achieve success, if you have the guts for risk and the fortitude for a real score.

And if you are financially successful, it will spill over and enrich your entire life.

EXPECT VOLATILITY

I get in the car to take my grandchildren for the four-hour drive up to the mountains and after driving three or four blocks, invariably one of them always asks, "Are we there yet?"

It would be nice if we could reach our goals so quickly, but unfortunately, things take time.

Brace yourself: In high-risk, high-return situations you will not find instant gratification. No one can promise wealth overnight. Nor when I talk about speculation do I mean quick trading profits.

The key to this game is patience. Wait for your special situation or opportunity. Then you must have backbone—the fortitude to sit through the extreme volatility, the up-and-down swings of a winner.

High-risk stocks are inherently unstable. They not only fluctuate, but often fluctuate violently. They can be extremely volatile because they are risky. You can run into an unfavorable article in *Barron's* or *Forbes* or any of the other financial journals. They gleefully knock these stocks. In fact, these publications feel a responsibility to do so because such stocks are obviously not yet proven commodities and so to the financial journals may seem quite obviously overpriced.

These stocks are not yet fiduciary holdings, that is, blue chips. It's hard for a journalist to write a terrible story about General Motors because GM is out there producing cars every day. The worst you can do with General Motors, perhaps, is to say that they are going to have a poor year or that the management is not outstanding.

But with young companies that rise in price as their story unfolds, the move may be so significant in attracting attention that it often prompts speculators to sell the stock short—that is, sell the stock without owning it, hoping to buy it back cheaper after it drops in price.

Then these very same short-sellers do their best to knock the stock down as much as possible so that they can maximize their profit. They call the news media and the journalists, who are interested in finding good ideas to knock and claim the stock is overpriced. The reporters, in a rush to meet their deadlines, feed on hot gossip and usually do only limited research, and some short-seller is happy to oblige them with all the negatives.

Bad news is something that people always love to hear. It makes good copy. I often buy these financial papers and magazines just to find out what they are knocking today and to see if they might be picking one of my favorite stocks. I buy these publications almost defensively.

These articles have only temporary effects. I have done well with stocks that the periodicals have rated poorly.

End of chpt 10

ELEVEN *goes to pg. 135 = 17 pgs.*

THE GREAT PYRAMIDS
OF WALL STREET

Investing in a stock is a lot like getting into a hot tub.

You start by sticking your toe in. If it feels good, you stick it in a little more and then submerge an entire foot. If it still feels good, you immerse yourself completely. If it starts to hurt, you pull out quick so you don't get burned.

I find the same holds true for a stock. If you start with a good feeling, if it makes money, buy more. Before you know it, you're pyramiding on the upside. Pyramiding is adding to your position at each new high. If you buy a stock at $15 and it goes to $25 and $30, don't pull out. Buy more of it at $25 and $30—it will probably go to $50. That's how you become very rich. That's how you become a millionaire.

With any meaningful amount—say you ultimately put in perhaps $50,000—you could be worth a couple of million dollars. With TIE/ Communications, which went from $6 to $269, you would have generated about forty-six times your initial investment. If you had put in $50,000, it would have been worth more than $2 million! That kind of opportunity is your rare chance to make it really big.

I'm not saying that you will always get to sell at the top; in fact, you almost never will. But even if you sold out halfway there, you would still have made over $1 million on $50,000. *That* is my point. To make these returns, you must pyramid.

If you pick a winner once in your life—Xerox or Genentech,

Compaq or Dell or Intel, Microsoft or Toys "R" Us—you'll love it and you'll make your fortune.

I LEARNED THE HARD WAY

Even up to very recently, I thought that in order to be successful and exceed the results of my peers—of other smart investors—I had to read and digest as much as possible of the financial information that is published ceaselessly every hour and every day of the week. I wanted to know more—indeed, know everything, every detail possible, every wriggle in the economic statistics, the unemployment rate and the inflation rate, the Consumer Price Index and the Producer Price Index, the Gross National Product and the Gross Domestic Product, the budget deficit and the trade deficit, the Federal Reserve's monetary numbers and interest rates, the Consumer Confidence Index and the Producer Confidence Index, the status of tax legislation, the federal government's fiscal policy, and what was happening to wages, the cost of goods—producer as well as consumer—and industry profit margins, and on and on. And all that was just to get a global frame of reference as to what the stock market might be likely to do. I was taught that I would be in a position to determine the probable direction in which the stock market would move by knowing and analyzing these numerous, varied, and complex economic and fiscal factors.

Collecting and reviewing the data was just the beginning. Then, of course, came the really big job that in essence required me to become a neurotically driven, overworked, computerlike individual, laboring to first gather and then analyze just about every industry's prospects based on the almost infinite outpouring of numbers that are inexorably disseminated (either to make us smarter, or maybe to bury us, to overwhelm us in their magnitude). Then finally and most importantly, I had to study, analyze, and evaluate (almost) every single company's past, present, and even projected future earnings, and to determine not only what multiple of earnings these companies were selling for, but indeed what multiples they should or would be selling at. I had to obtain, subscribe to, and send away for every research analyst's report to learn what other, perhaps wiser, individuals had concluded about each of these industries and individual companies. The work was constant and overwhelming; it was like being on a treadmill that never stopped and, in fact, seemed always to be speeding up, as I was privileged to become the beneficiary of ever more comprehensive, detailed, and voluminous information.

But I had no choice. I was driven to succeed, no matter the price I had to pay. No effort would be too great. If I could just digest all this encyclopedic information and process it through my brain, I felt that given the fortunate benefit of my Harvard Business School education, I couldn't miss, and that I had an absolute formula for success in the stock market.

Indeed, in several cases I did such intensive and extensive research that I probably knew as much about the company I was analyzing as its President or Chairman of the Board. Notwithstanding my dedicated effort and comprehensive knowledge, I found that I was still unable, based on this type of analysis, to determine with consistency what a stock would be selling for in the future.

I have finally learned the total hopelessness of this intensive yet counterproductive approach. One gets buried by too much information. You not only blow your time, but you blow out your brain. You often tend to become fixated on minutiae—all interesting, all even relevant—but, unfortunately, all that effort doesn't tell you which way the market is going to go or which way a given stock is going to go.

It was precisely the fact that I commonly knew more about a company than nearly anyone else, yet still couldn't predict how the company's stock would perform, which led me to develop a different and relatively simple investment strategy. I began to see that the price action of a stock is actually the best predictor of what the stock will be selling for in the future, and more specifically, that a new high in a stock is the best indicator that the stock will subsequently sell at an even higher price. So today I advocate an investment strategy of buying a stock when it hits a new high and pyramiding (buying more stock) as the price continues to rise. In this chapter, I spell out the basis for this investment strategy and how to implement it. Follow the strategy and you'll be on your way to making your own fortune.

SIMPLE INVESTMENT IDEAS WORK

Thankfully, and indeed luckily for you—and I have now come to learn for me, too—life is simple! We ourselves tend to make it more complex than it is or need be. Likewise, the stock market is simple. We make it much more complex than it is. As I describe below, the biggest winners—the Warren Buffetts, the Benjamin Grahams and David Dodds, and the Peter Lynches of the world—operated and achieved the immense successes that they did because they each locked on to a simple idea and tenaciously adhered to it.

In the case of Warren Buffett, his idea was to identify and buy the stocks of the great brand name companies. They have the foothold, the leadership, the franchises—like Coca-Cola—that will ultimately command an ever-larger following with an ever-growing world audience that will produce ever-growing profits and thereby achieve substantially enhanced value for the company's shareholders. It's a simple idea. It's brilliant in its simplicity. Yes, it does require some selective, intelligent, sometimes even incisive analysis to identify these companies. But once you know what you're looking for—what your theme is—it's almost too simple.

In the case of Benjamin Graham and David Dodd—the fathers of the contrarian school of investing—their idea was simple, too. They would analyze financial statements of public companies, and, since markets are imperfect, they would look for companies whose public prices did not reflect their true underlying worth. As Mario Gabelli, a more recent and outstandingly successful money manager applying

Graham and Dodd's strategies might say, such companies did not reflect their actual "private market value." In other words, if you accumulated a position in these momentarily misvalued—or in the analysis of Graham and Dodd and Gabelli, undervalued—situations, you would in due course realize immense gains once others came to appreciate the real worth of such companies.

In the case of Peter Lynch, the brilliant former manager of the Magellan Fund who produced such fabulous results over many years running a large accumulation of other peoples' money, he did it in a way that I am proud to say I myself lectured on as early as thirty-five years ago. In a subsequent chapter of this book entitled "The Best Advice is Free," I describe in full the strategy Lynch applied. In short, Lynch achieved great investing success just by finding out what products homemakers and mothers—the most important consumers and spenders in our society—were buying for themselves and for their families. Invest in the companies that make these products. It's that simple.

THE TREND IS YOUR FRIEND

The simplest idea of all, and best idea of all, because it will help you jump on every winner that Warren Buffett or Peter Lynch or any of the great money managers, past or future, will ever buy, is, as I discuss in this chapter—to buy the new highs. If you do that, they, these so-called geniuses, indeed these true geniuses based on their records, have essentially identified for you the stocks you should buy.

If I did all of the time what I am now telling you to do—no, what I am urging you to do—I'd have been many, many times more successful and made far fewer costly and painful mistakes. You see, based on my earlier intensive and extensive hard work and research, day and night, scanning, reading, and studying, I often concluded that a stock was selling at too high a price, so I'd sell the stock (if I already owned it) or short it with the view that I would achieve a greater overall profit by getting out of the stock.

Forget it! The best analysis—the most comprehensive, all-knowing, or more accurately, best-knowing, destination of any stock—is the very clear, right-in-front-of-your-face, unfolding behavior of that stock. If a stock is very strong, if it is moving up, jump on it. You need not be a genius. Just follow the basic law of physics that says a moving object will keep moving in the same direction until some external force comes along and either stops it or reverses it.

A stock on the way up will keep moving up and a stock that is moving down will keep moving down. Jump on a stock that is doing well. Then, as in a poker game, if you have a bad experience, step out and take your losses. If you have a good experience, stay and add to it.

It's so hard to find an outstanding winner that when you find one, play it for all it's worth. Always ride a winner until it shows signs that it's no longer a winner. Capitalize on this law, this truism. Pyramid and buy on the way up. Add to your position at each new high, because pyramiding on the upside is an invaluable discipline, a winning formula.

One of my best moves—buying Doubleday at a time when it wasn't making any money worth speaking of—was based on this very strategy. I had always been a fan of the Mets, which Doubleday owned, and I kept pyramiding on the upside because the stock kept acting well. I ended up making $13 million. I put up less than $3 million and within two years got back more than $16 million just by pyramiding the winner. True, the amount I invested is not for the average investor, but anyone could have put up any comfortable amount and made the better than 400 percent return that I did by following the same strategy.

My criteria in that case were almost the opposite from what I usually use. Almost without exception, I do intensive research into a company, but in this particular case, I had no communication with Doubleday management; I met with them only once, to find out if they were willing to sell the Mets to me. Doubleday wasn't showing much in earnings, but I liked the stock action. I invested just by watching the stock and seeing it move up—making new highs. As it moved up, I kept adding to it enough to make a big play and a tremendous gain.

The Mets became more valuable over the longer term. Then a German company, Bertelsmann, took over the publishing division, which sustained good underlying ingredients and value. Those elements, apparently, were reflected in the stock action—as it moved up for no obvious reason.

BUY HIGH, SELL HIGHER

Even now, knowing what I know and knowing from experience that it's the smart thing to do, I still find buying at the high very hard. Psychologically, it goes against the grain. It's like entering new, unexplored territory. Each time you buy at a new high you feel like the first idiot who paid this high price.

If the range was $16 to $40 it's easy to buy it if it's down to $20. But if the range was $16 to $40 and you pay $40.50, you ask yourself, "What if I'm paying the ultimate high? What if it never hits that price again?" As panic sinks in, you feel as if you are the Greater Fool—the last buyer, the guy with no one to sell to, the one to whom everybody else has already sold his stock at a huge profit.

If you do buy a stock and it moves up and you finally get a chance to cash out with a good profit, it's hard to let your profits ride and even harder to invest more money at another new high. The natural human tendency is to grab your profit for fear you may lose your cherished gain—something that is, realistically, always a possibility. The vast majority of investors prefer to take the money and run and you will fight with yourself to make this daring decision, risking what you already have to buy more and pyramid your gains.

But your move can be well worth it, for these highs often go dramatically higher, usually for sound yet unknown reasons.

When I talk about buying new highs, I am referring to the Big Board, the stocks listed on the New York and American Stock Exchanges and Nasdaq with established trading ranges. When they break through to new highs, it means something happened that changed their prospects for growth.

Remember this: If you always followed this strategy and bought at new highs, you would own every major winner, because almost every single company that was ever taken over hit the new-high list before it was bought out.

By pyramiding, you would have put yourself in a position to participate in nearly every corporate takeover that occurred—as well as every great growth stock—from Compaq to Intel to Toys "R" Us to Microsoft—well before it made its major move, well before its greatest capital appreciation actually occurred.

Once in a very great while, winning stocks *don't* hit new highs. But generally, the stocks break out because someone knows important news is pending. Significant or magnificent, new developments occur. By following that lead, you will pick up the same winning stock without any inside information. I urge my clients to do it and I do it myself.

Best of all, it's so easy to do. It's a no-brainer. So buy the new highs!

LOWS GO LOWER

Of course, some people really like to buy new lows. There's a popular dictum that says you get rich by buying low and selling high. That's obviously true, but it's also very hard to do. What can happen is that you buy low and the stock goes lower and lower. Generally it is low because there is something terrible happening in the company. The company may even go bankrupt. Nobody knows what "low" really is, except in retrospect.

As one brilliant money manager once succinctly said in advising against buying into a declining stock—"The one thing you want to avoid catching is a falling knife. It can kill you. And buying a falling stock, though it is seductive because it looks so cheap, can kill you too."

When I first entered the market, I also looked for new lows. I was nineteen and my brother was almost eighteen. In our naïveté—what we considered at the time our "genius"—we thought we discovered a new formula. We said, "Well, this stock was $40 and it's now $16. It's got to be a good buy at $16. And it's easy to buy. It's a real bargain." We thought we would automatically be winners because the stock was so much higher. It seemed like a "can't-miss" cinch.

We bought the new lows.

Then we found, to our dismay, that the new lows led to even newer lows and for very good reasons. The companies were generally in serious trouble.

We weren't big players in those days; we bought maybe 100 shares of each stock. Fortunately, we quickly learned that our formula was not the secret to making a fortune—in fact, maybe quite the reverse. Just as new highs often lead to newer highs in the future, new lows often herald only newer lows. In retrospect, it was worthwhile experimenting with this strategy, though we hardly thought so at the time. We wanted to make money and we wound up losing a significant part of our principal.

WHERE IS THE TOP?

Selling high isn't so easy, either, because the hardest decision, as most professionals will tell you, is deciding when to sell. Professionals can pick stocks, but they don't know any better than you do when to get out. Almost nobody knows where the top is.

Sometimes you sell too early and you're ready to kill yourself because then—of course!—a really big move occurs. So the thing to do and the way to make money in the market no matter how hard it is, is to be disciplined and keep pyramiding as the stock goes up.

Do this as long as the stock keeps on doing well and protect yourself with a stop loss. Then keep raising the price of your stop-loss sell order even if it's only a form of insurance. If the stock suddenly suffers a 10 percent or maximum 15 percent drop, you must get out. You may not get out at the top, but at least you'll protect most of your profits.

It is a tough discipline to follow. Even as I strongly advise this sound strategy, I must confess that very much to my financial chagrin, occasionally I don't follow my own advice. Psychologically, you get sucked in. You want to be a winner, you liked it higher, so certainly you don't want to unload the position 15 percent down. You rationalize; you hope; you believe; you wish. And then you find you're down 20 percent and then 25 percent and it's either just too big a loss—or even a loss of profits in some cases—and you decide to stay in just a little longer waiting for the bounce that never comes or, if it comes, it's just a temporary interval before a new dive and you really get killed. So, as I suggested, stop out at 10 percent or 15 percent down and pay this insurance against a really damaging loss. At least once you are out you can be objective. You will no longer be emotionally involved. You will no longer be married to the situation, so you can step back and look, and if you decide you still like the stock, you can buy it back—based on a new, separate decision.

First, follow the rule: If it drops 15 percent don't vacillate. Get out. Protect your profits in the case where you rode the stock up for a big gain and stop your losses, at least limit them, in the case where you are losing on the stock. It's a really tough discipline to follow consistently. Sometimes you stop out at 10 percent or 15 percent down and it turns right around and goes up another 80 percent. Then you feel like an idiot and mistrust this approach.

But in the market, we all play probabilities. No one is right all the time—not even the top performers.

A WINNING FORMULA

I'm not saying that this strategy always works; nothing always works. If it did, everyone would soon come to know it and follow it and everybody would be immensely rich and obviously only a select few are. But it's a good guide to detecting winners or potential winners. Picking good stocks isn't really hard, because in a very real sense they select themselves. They reveal themselves through their price action. They can't keep it a secret, they announce themselves because they suddenly make new highs and the volume picks up. That pattern is easy to follow.

Latch onto a trend! Because a behavior pattern always shows up in the new highs listings, had you followed this almost too simple approach you would have latched onto the fabulous run-ups of the conglomerates in the 1960s, the new issue market of the late '60s, the takeovers and leveraged buyouts of the '80s, the biotechs and computer software and the small cap stocks of the late '80s and early '90s. You would have identified an emerging trend, a vogue, and the emerging winners, and you would have owned them and made the really big gains that can really build one's fortune.

My motto? Buy high and sell *higher.* When you buy new highs, it means that somebody identified something that says, "This thing is going higher." You are jumping on a trend.

What I am giving you here are the best suggestions about the probabilities and the formulas that work best. This is the strategy that works for some of the top performing pros. This is the strategy that worked for me the greatest number of times.

THE LOGIC OF BUYING AT THE NEW HIGH

Just think about it. At any given moment in time all shares are selling in the market at a price that reflects fully all the knowledge as it is known by each and every "player" about each company. Every day, and even over the course of many days, the overwhelming majority of stocks trade within a relatively narrow range—neither significantly breaking out into new highs nor breaking down to new lows. When shares break out of these narrow ranges by, for example, hitting a new high, you may justifiably assume that something meaningful is happening with the company that is instigating such a breakout.

The new high itself gives the observant, alert investor a very tangible, unequivocal signal that something significant may be happening, and it is this clear, unavoidable, impossible-to-hide, flashing signal that is your instant signal to act—to jump on the bandwagon, so to speak, and participate in this outbreak, this momentum that generated the new high. If you are even minimally awake, you can't miss it, because it's like exploding fireworks on a clear night. Your financial newspaper will highlight that "new high" for you in the morning paper, or you can even program your computer to signal any such new highs during the trading day while the markets are open.

Buying at the new high also makes logical sense because of the momentum implicit in the flow of funds from investors, particularly institutional investors. The movement of the stock market both up and down depends in large part on this flow of funds. When funds are going into stocks, as opposed to other investments, the stock market will generally move up, and conversely, when funds are going out of stocks, the stock market will generally move down. New highs often indicate that the flow of funds is moving aggressively into the specific issues achieving the new highs. For example, six issues—Microsoft, Intel, Cisco, Oracle, Coca-Cola, and General Electric—made nearly continuous new highs for the period from 1991 to 1997, as mutual funds and other institutions persistently bought these stocks. Recently, the phenomenon of investing in stocks that are riding a bull market has even been given a name; it's called "momentum investing." But the explosive growth in the price of such popular stocks, which cannot be justified purely on the basis of book value or P/E ratios, is really just a function of the flow of investment funds exceeding the supply of the most popular stocks. Accordingly, the new highs are often indicative of where the flow of funds is focused.

So try buying the new highs. You'll like it. You'll thank me. Can anything be any clearer, simpler, and potentially, and in my judgment, more rewarding than buying the new highs? For heaven's sake, and for yours, don't vacillate—go to it now!

QUITE CONTRARY

There is more than one way to make money in the market. Another very good formula is to be a contrarian investor. When everybody is bullish, you get out of the market. When everybody is bearish, you sit there and accumulate. Any formula that works is obviously a good formula.

I remember one client, an elderly gentleman, who used the contrarian formula exactly once each year. He used to come in on November 15 each year and play the market. Right through the end of December, he bought every stock that was under tax-selling pressure, every stock that was down and was being beaten down even further by year-end tax selling.

This man was phenomenal; such discipline! The rest of the year he was out of the market. He never called me, never traded. His portfolio contained some good stocks that he never sold. But he picked only stocks that were depressed during the year and that became even more depressed at the end of the year because of the general urgency people feel to sell in order to realize tax losses. So he would buy only from November 15 to December 31, the last day of tax selling. Over the next sixty days, he sold out all of those stocks. He used to average, every year, a more than 30 percent return for just that one-and-a-half-month period. If you annualize that figure, it would be about 240 percent a year. The important thing is that he was disciplined.

There is an inordinate amount of selling at year-end, propelled by the need to sell by December 31 to realize tax losses for the year and take advantage of the tax savings. For the most part, people—by nature it seems—just don't do it any earlier. At the same time, there is no commensurate compelling reason to buy that will offset their selling until right after January 1, when many of the same people who sold their stock buy back their positions. Moreover, the mere fact that the inordinate selling pressure stopped makes it easy for the stock to bounce back, without much volume, to where it should be or would have been, before the tax selling.

By taking advantage of this disproportionate amount of seasonal selling, this elderly gentleman established a formula and a discipline that worked for him. In fact, this phenomenon recently earned a name, the "January Effect." If somebody wants to take the time, this is a fabulous formula for making money. Moreover, being a contrarian can pay off in terms of realizing substantial gains in market timing. When everyone loves the market, when the bullish sentiment is very strong, it's probably a smart time to sell. Yes, there may be more upside left but at that juncture the risks on the downside outweigh the rewards on the upside.

Remember, you are in the market to make money over time, to play the probabilities and try to be right more often than you are wrong. Not to be absolutely right—nobody ever is, nobody ever will be. If you act contrarian, you can be a big winner over time.

When everybody loved gold it topped $800 an ounce and made the front pages of *The New York Times*. That's generally a good sign it's over and a great time to get out—or a good time to short it if you have the inclination and audaciousness to play that side of the market.

Likewise, when everybody hates the market and is panicking, that is the time to be a contrarian and step in and buy aggressively. Remember the 1987 crash? The Dow Jones dropped more than 500 points in one day. The next morning people panicked again. Contrarians stepped in that morning or any time later that week and achieved dramatic, even phenomenal, gains over the next two to three years.

When investors are very optimistic, almost everyone is a buyer and consequently individuals and institutions are already fully invested. The market is way up and expectations are high, so anything less than ensuing, very positive good news leads to a sharp market drop. The corollary is that when investors' moods are very depressed, nobody wants to buy. They all want to hold their cash. They've thrown in the towel on equities, the market is way down, and they're braced for poor or even disastrous results. So even moderately decent news can be a pleasant surprise and lead to a significant market rise.

Don't follow the sheep. If you want to be king, be courageous like the lions. Move in aggressively where and when others fear to tread.

FUNDAMENTALIST INVESTING

I know some investors, such as Warren Buffett, who make money by following contrarian investment philosophy, first articulated in Benjamin Graham's seminal book, *The Intelligent Investor*, the bible of contrarian investment. The essence of the Graham and Dodd school is looking at the fundamental, underlying value of a company, rather than emphasizing diversification across companies and industries. These contrarians argue, "If you can buy value, if you can buy a dollar for 80 cents, you'll make money." So they buy strong balance sheets, strong companies, and never pay more than the book value—the private market value or the intrinsic value of the company. Preferably, when they can, they pay much less. How much cash does the company have, how much liability?

Investors who follow that formula do very well, because if you buy good value—which incidentally becomes abundantly available during sharp market breaks like the panic selling in the crash of 1987—if you buy great companies at discounts to their net worth or, in extremes, their cash or liquidation value, in due course you will see potential takeover situations and great profits. When the market is doing poorly, when investors are running scared, I often buy some stocks that sell below their liquidating value. Following this single strategy, Warren Buffett scooped up bargains in numerous bear markets.

Those were timing and opportunity situations resulting from cycles in the stock market. Because of the psychology of the time related to the bear market brought about by the oil crisis, good stocks were extremely depressed. They sold at prices substantially below the replacement value of their assets, liquidation value, or their potential earning power. Look for these situations, because even so-called good stocks can be bad buys if quality is the only yardstick and the timing is wrong and the stocks are already overpriced.

Even with good stocks, though you can make money on them if you time them right, you can also lose a lot on them, no matter how well they're rated, if your timing is off.

The problem with the fundamentalist approach is that sometimes a company just looks cheap. It may sell at a discount to its book value, but that bargain may be more apparent than real.

So choose one of the strategies outlined in this chapter:

- **Pyramid**: Observe a substantial increase in a stock's volume and particularly its breakout in price to new highs and then buy more at subsequent new highs.

- **Contrarian**: Accumulate positions and be bullish when market sentiment is overly negative and selling positions when market sentiment is overly positive.

- **Fundamentalist**: Research and buy companies that are trading at substantial discounts to their cash or liquidation values.

End of chpt. II

Chpt TWELVE ⟩ goes to pg. 147 = 11 pgs.

THE DANGERS OF SAFETY

If I make only one essential point for all investors, aggressive and conservative, it is that there is no such thing as a safe stock.

There is a joke about an airplane crashing into the ocean approximately one mile offshore. All the passengers exited atop the wing, and just as the plane began sinking the pilot loudly announced, "All those who have life preservers, put them on and start heading for shore; all those who can swim, please swim toward shore. The rest of you, we want to thank you for flying our airline."

For me, this little joke encapsulates the atmosphere of the stock market. Many investors are fairly well equipped, cruising along safely, but unfortunately there are always those who are left behind, on the losing end. You must always be aware that though you can make a fortune in the stock market, there is also an element of real risk.

Even so-called safe stocks are not safe. In fact, there is a greater, hidden risk in many of the blue chips or so-called fiduciary stocks, because you pay a significant premium—close to top dollar—for top performance and top reputation.

What I recommend goes contrary to what the public, many of the professional money managers, and the business writers and industry regulators generally advocate.

The investment establishment makes blue chips the "safe" way to play. If brokers or money managers recommend the buy of a young, relatively unknown company and their clients lose money, they will be criticized and even sued on the contention that they failed to do their fiduciary duty.

By contrast, if the same brokers lose money for their clients with blue chips, they are much less likely to be criticized or censured. No one can say they had no right to recommend AT&T or U.S. Steel (now USX), because there's a pile of documentation around telling you why you should buy it. Even if the brokers prove wrong and lose money for their clients, there is always some massive and extensive body of research to justify their mistake.

After more than thirty-five years on the firing line, I have observed that over an extended period of time, the blue chips carry great risk—sometimes more risk than equities lacking their privileged ranking.

No one else to my recollection makes this point and it is an important one to stress, especially in markets in which everyone buys blue chips either at outlandish prices or in a so-called flight to quality. The stock market collapse in October 1987 reminded us of the fragility of the market, as a trillion dollars' worth of wealth was destroyed in a flashing sweep. Public investors and professional money managers need always be alert to that threat, lest they become comfortable and lull themselves into passivity or false security.

This is true not only for technical reasons, but from a fundamental point of view. Never assume you are buying safety and need not watch your investment. When you pay for safety, you generally are paying absolute top dollar, without much upside potential. Not always, but generally.

An excellent, albeit tragic example are the many investors in the rock solid, so-called riskless investment in Lloyd's of London, the biggest and best-known casualty insurance company in the world. Becoming a Lloyd's "name," as the investors are called, was considered a privileged ticket, an opportunity to achieve outstanding financial returns. It was a virtual ticket into the upper echelon of British society where wealthy Americans put their fortunes.

In recent years Lloyd's was rocked by huge losses from a series of man-made and natural disasters, as well as by poor management. The "names," being unlimited partners, were asked to pay up sometimes to the tune of their entire wealth. At least four "names," very elite and formerly very wealthy, committed suicide, and hundreds of others faced the possible loss of their retirement funds, family heirlooms, homes, and nearly everything else they owned. The personal family anguish that the "names" went through was horrendous. In fact, at least two dozen Members of Parliament who themselves had invested in Lloyd's faced devastating losses from their "sure thing" investment in the troubled insurance company.

It must be clearly understood that over the years, no investment was considered safer, more desirable, or more rewarding than becoming a "name" in Lloyd's.

So much for the riskless "sure thing." Remember, whenever you think you've invested in a sure thing, a false sense of security keeps you from being as careful as you otherwise would be and watching your investment as closely as you would any high-risk situation. You become relaxed, complacent, even lethargic. Then, because of your comfort level, you may absorb enormous capital deterioration before you realize what hit you or before you even understand what a high risk it was that you really took. Always remember that risk is a question of expectation and expectation is a function of current reality, which may differ greatly from past reality, and of human psychology. These things fluctuate wildly, especially in an age of change.

WHERE ARE THE STARS OF YESTERYEAR?

When I came into the market in 1959, just starting out as a broker, everybody told me to "buy the blue chips," the fiduciary stocks, the "widows-and-orphans" stocks.

Back in the go-go years of the late '60s and early '70s, the blue chips were called "no decision" or "no-brainer" stocks. You weren't required to think about them. You knew that if you bought the Dow thirty or the "favorite fifty" of the large institutions, you just couldn't lose. You bought Polaroid, you bought Control Data, you bought the entire list of Dow Jones stocks. Control Data was at an all-time high in 1967 at over $160, and Polaroid reached its high in 1969 at over $145. Several years later, these stocks were among the market's worst performers. Polaroid ultimately dropped to as low as $14 a share. Control Data plummeted as low as $10.

I vividly remember being in the boardroom the day in 1959 when U.S. Steel reached a new all-time high of $100 a share. Everybody cheered! The people on the floor of the New York Stock Exchange broke open champagne. That was a triple-A stock, one of the bluest of the blue chips. By 1993, U.S. Steel was $43.

If you weren't a widow or orphan to begin with, you would have become one by owning and holding U.S. Steel. It was, in fact, a tragic investment!

If U.S. Steel were unique, I'd say there was no point in mentioning it. But the safe widows-and-orphans stocks, "the blue chips," recommended in that day included Johns-Manville Corporation, which later declared bankruptcy; International Harvester, another major company that almost went into bankruptcy and that required a major restructuring; and United Fruit, a company once so powerful that if someone attacked one of its fruit or banana farms—in South America, for example—the United States would send down an American battleship. The country in question would immediately establish United Fruit's clear title and there would be no more trouble. United Fruit never went into bankruptcy, but it came close to it and is still rebuilding. Had you bought it in its halcyon days, you would have lost tons of money—not to mention the aggravation you would have gone through.

The recommended investment list of these days also included what were then considered the safe outstanding blue chips at the time, such as the Pennsylvania Railroad and the New York Central Railroad, both of which subsequently—you guessed it—went into bankruptcy. The list included all of the steel companies—Kayser, Bethlehem, Youngstown, Republic, Jones and Laughlin. All were blue chips. So were the copper companies—Kennecott, Anaconda, and Kaiser Aluminum. Western Union was also a member of this blue chip, so-called safe category. Other members of the club included utilities and department stores such as Macy's.

Those "blue chips" weren't disasters—they were spectacular disasters.

WHY BUY JUNK?

The same phenomenon occurred in the bond market.

Unproven, riskier bonds, like yet-to-be-proven, riskier stocks, yielded a superior total return to that of the safe triple-A bonds.

Today, largely because of Michael Milken's "success"—or rather, his missionary zeal—in pioneering high-yield junk bond offerings at Drexel Burnham, there's a new attitude toward high-risk bonds. Milken, as you will recall, was a financial superstar brought down for insider trading and sent to jail.

Milken's theory was that the high returns of these lower-grade debt instruments more than compensated for the risk of default they posed.

There's a lot to be said for that position. Between 1900 and 1943, even including the Depression years, only 1.7 percent of all straight public and private debt defaulted. And between 1980 and 1984, the annual default rate on straight corporate debt was less than 0.5 percent.

About fifteen years before Milken did the research that made junk bonds respectable, my younger brother, Philip, made the same observations in his doctoral thesis at the Harvard Business School. He found that you were better off buying lower-grade bonds than you were double- or triple-As. Over the prior fifty years, you would have achieved a significantly better overall return from lower-grade bonds than from those with the highest ratings.

Why? Because when you buy triple-As and accept the lower yield they provide, you are assuming that they're safe because they're top quality.

Yet, having achieved these A to AAA ratings, these bonds have nowhere to go in order to get any safer. Nowhere to go but down, that is, and many in fact have declined or even defaulted.

Johns-Manville, International Harvester, and some of the utilities—many of the bluest of blue-chip companies, all formerly rated A to AAA—ran into financial trouble. And many former blue-chip companies don't even exist today. The issuers of low-grade bonds paid higher rates to compensate for their seemingly higher risk. This initial interest rate premium, plus the possibility of upgrading, made the return of lower-grade bonds attractive. Between January 1982 and May 1984, if you bought a portfolio of high-yield bonds, you would have gotten an average return of 20.3 percent a year, instead of 16.6 percent on A-rated bonds and 15 percent on triple-As. Lower-quality bonds also often turn out to be less volatile or risky, as many investors define risk, than higher-grade issues.

Lower-rated bonds, although some issuers have experienced bankruptcies, nevertheless overall have provided significantly higher returns that have more than compensated for their greater risk. The higher yields of these instruments more than made up for the bankruptcies and misfortunes of these small or riskier companies. Of course, in some cases companies went under because they over-burdened themselves with excessive debt.

Moreover, some of these risky companies grew and improved to the point where they themselves achieved an A or triple-A rating and went up in price in accord with their new, improved ratings. In the end, despite the initial risks, these lower-rated "junk bonds" turned out to be the better investments.

Paradoxically, with success came excess. In their early years, high-yield or junk bonds were of comparatively higher quality and more rare. But with increasing acceptance and growing popularity throughout the 1980s, they were occasionally used to finance deals of marginal economic merit—overpriced acquisitions which could not support the debt load they took on and thus were doomed to fail. Such overly high-priced deals reached in some cases excessive and dangerous proportions in the late 1980s. But then again, that's what business risk is all about—stock can become very overpriced as public expectations of the company's success outdistance reality and so can businessmen's expectations of future revenues to service their high-yielding bonds. Generally speaking, however, companies don't take on debt willy-nilly. Since anything may happen in a stock market driven by consumer expectations and psychology, common stock remains, on average, much riskier than so-called junk bonds. Again, the greater the risk, though, the greater the potential for reward.

In fact, the increasing popularity of junk bonds undercut the very basis of the research study that Milken did for documenting the superior performance of lower-graded over top-quality bonds. Before ubiquitous junk, lower-graded bonds were called junk precisely because their issuers were less financially strong than the triple-A to double-A and single-A issuers. Because they were perceived as weaker, these companies were permitted to issue only a very limited volume of debt.

However, seeing the high returns for relatively low risk these instruments afforded, people clamored for more. Demand by all sorts of investors for junk bonds skyrocketed—savings and loans, commercial banks, institutional investors, pension funds, and specialized mutual funds were formed specifically to buy these junk bonds. With such demand, the pressure was on to create supply—and the volume and the percentage of debt issued became overwhelming and unprecedented.

Never have so many businesses, with so little to warrant it in the economic fundamentals, been so heavily leveraged.

The resulting business risk thus became much greater than in the past with the earlier low-rated, high yielding bonds. The "junkiness" was magnified.

In other words, these new buyers, institutions as well as individuals, were not buying the product they thought they were buying, the relatively low-risk but high-yielding bonds that historically produced such superior returns. Because of their sudden fantastic popularity and the market's almost fanatical belief that such bonds would produce a superior return, the amount of debt that marginal companies were suddenly able to issue got to the point where the risks became far greater than that which such bonds historically carried. Accordingly, one result of the net increase in highly leveraged corporate structures, through junk bonds, will be more defaults when the inevitable economic recessions occur—even, perhaps, during very mild ones or, for very highly leveraged companies, just moderate slowdowns.

YOUNG BLOOD

Contrary to what the public and many professional money managers believe, once everybody accepts a company and believes in its future, its credibility, acceptability, and reputation are already reflected in the stock price. This, therefore, leaves it very little room to go up. Microsoft was a great exception, because it operates in growth areas related to information technology and productivity and because it consistently stays on top of technology, without getting fat and lazy, as so often occurs with big companies.

However, any company with an established reputation is generally a mature company. When you buy a mature company, its performance is sometimes analogous to what happens to an elderly person. They suffer from a slowing of growth, a rigidity, and lack of the flexibility and drive so essential to moving forward quickly in an ever-competitive race. For companies so afflicted, I call it "hardening of the corporate bureaucratic arteries."

It is like the joke about the ninety-year-old man who was sitting on a park bench crying.

A policeman came along and asked him why he was crying. He

said, "Last week I married a young girl. She's beautiful, she's a great dancer, she's sweet and enticing." "So what's wrong?" asked the policeman. "I can't remember my way home."

Mature companies ultimately lose their direction and inspiration, the dynamic energetic leadership that young companies have in abundance. They lose their tenacity, their dreams. They forget what made them successful to begin with. They lose the venturesome, innovative people who make excitement and drama. They become overweight, top-heavy with management, and layered in bureaucracy.

At that point, of course, mature companies become extremely vulnerable and their stocks fall apart.

From a very broad perspective, this vulnerability is healthy.

This process is akin to what the famous Harvard economist Joseph Schumpeter called "creative destruction," in which the competitiveness of capitalism constantly causes inefficient companies to restructure—and in the process builds new opportunities. New companies emerge. This is why takeovers or threats of takeovers and corporate reorganizations are often helpful—as painful as they may be for the people involved who must adjust to the new reality by finding and learning a new job. Restructuring under new management—or the threat of it happening—forces a company to change, reawaken, restructure, and move forward or else go under.

It reminds me of a story about the late Branch Rickey, the general manager of the Brooklyn Dodgers in the 1940s.

After many years of being in last place, the Dodgers finally won the National League pennant in the summer of 1947. The ensuing winter, Rickey traded some of the very players who helped achieve that miraculous accomplishment. The sports writers asked him, "How can you break up a team that won a championship?"

He wisely responded to the effect that "You can't stand still. If you accept the status quo, you inevitably fall backwards. You must act to stay in the lead. If you don't move forward you move backwards."

In life, even at the very height of success, you cannot rest on your laurels. Each day you must act. You must make new, difficult decisions that inevitably entail risk but will hopefully bring new successes.

The most essential rule if you manage your own money is that the only chance of safety is by staying on top of your investments or choosing someone brilliant or someone you have faith in—preferably someone who is both—to stay on top of them for you.

A Wall of Worry

There is risk in safety—and there is safety in risk.

In fact, I actually feel that there is more safety in buying risky stocks. It is often said that for the market to go up, it must climb a wall of worry. So it is with stocks. Stocks go up in the face of uncertainty—as fears about their prospects dissipate.

Once a stock is a sure thing, everybody already knows, loves, and owns it. There is no one left to buy it. Then something unexpected occurs and everyone runs to the window and sells at once. That's when we see the dramatic price drops. Everyone felt they were safe. They paid for that quality, that safety and security. And that's the biggest danger, that you felt the blue chips were safe and wanted to stay with them, emotionally, even though the facts might be indicating that the tide had turned.

Mark Twain had the right idea. He wisely advised against all conventional wisdom that diversification leads to better results, against the old maxim, not to put all your eggs in one basket. "Do," Twain urged, "put all your eggs in one basket—and watch that basket closely."

Diversification is not a solution to risk, as some investors believe.

If you invest your money all over the place, you will only get an average result. You may as well buy mutual funds, because once you are extensively diversified, it will be hard to outperform the averages.

You will have some winners and some losers. What's worse is that when the market goes down, your stocks will all go down together.

So, too, when the market goes bad, it takes the good stocks along with the losers. When the market turned sour in 1973–74, sure things collapsed and did even worse than the others.

If you are going to be in a risk game, which is what the stock market is, then you must recognize and acknowledge—in fact, embrace—the risk. Instead of buying stocks all over the place, take 70 percent of your funds and put them in gilt-edged U.S. Government Treasury notes or securities. That's your safety, that's your security. Then, with a smaller amount of your money, take a much bigger risk and go for the big rewards.

Most people do something different. They take 100 percent of their money and, often, even go on margin, hoping to double their profits and get rich quick. For example, with $100,000 on 50 percent margin, they can buy $200,000 worth of stock. If the stock doubles, they think they'll make $200,000 instead of only $100,000. What happens too often is that the $200,000 worth of stock they bought goes down 50 percent and is worth only $100,000. Since they have to give back the borrowed $100,000, they lose their entire investment. They are completely wiped out.

Be smart. Don't go on margin, because then you can be totally ruined. There is a famous Wall Street saying, "He who invests what isn't his must pay it back or go to prison." It makes much more sense to take the bigger, calculated risk with a small part of your portfolio. Take 30 percent of your funds or whatever portion you want to risk and be very aggressive. If you can make 300 percent on that 30 percent, that is an exciting strategy and meanwhile you will feel a greater sense of security because you are not risking everything.

Once you've decided what you want to risk, let it roll. Make your best decision, study all the angles first and go for it! But make sure you stay on top of it. Do not throw all your eggs in one basket. Put some eggs carefully in one basket and then watch that basket very closely. This is really the better and ultimately safer approach.

End of Chpt. 12

chpt. 13

THIRTEEN ⟩ goe to pg. 159 = 1 fys

TIME AND TIME AGAIN

A guy was walking down the street and asked another guy what time it was.

"It's three o'clock" was the polite reply.

"Thank you," says the first guy. "It's strange but I've been asking that question all day long and each time I get a different answer."

Knowing the right time is important because there's a right time to buy and a right time to sell. In order to make big gains, you must take big risks. But you want to limit your risk and protect your capital by knowing when to sell so that you don't get completely wiped out. Try selling at a point when you can limit your losses to about 15 percent or some other fixed maximum, so that you won't find it too hard to get back at least to even again.

If you buy a stock at $10 and it drops 15 percent, you still have $8.50 to work with. And if you make a 20 percent gain from there, you are back at about $10. But if you let it drop 50 percent, you must double your money just to get even and that's not easy.

So it is important to protect yourself against major losses when you take these positions. You must do so even though a stock may drop that 15 percent and then rebound for a 500 percent gain. You still must make sure that you don't let something wipe you out. And one stock *can* wipe you out.

Two principles are involved here.

Capital preservation is the first and taking advantage of whatever tax benefits you can glean is the second.

At year's end, I take tax losses because it is well worth it. If you put $20,000 into a stock and you lose $10,000, then the minute you sell it, that $10,000 loss is reduced by your tax saving. If you are in the 40 percent bracket, you immediately made back $4,000 of your loss. It also forces you to discipline yourself to take losses. This is a very effective strategy for me and it got me out of many bad stocks.

ACTIONS SPEAK LOUDER THAN WORDS

One important practice I followed over the years is not relying exclusively on everything management or people who own large blocks of stock tell you. Management people have a vested interest in the price of their stock and they usually believe in their company, on an emotional level. People who own large blocks of stock also have a vested interest in their performance.

Many people promote stocks because they own them and want other people to push the stocks up so that they can get out. That is true of brokerage firms, although it is less true these days. Still, many brokers with a big position in a stock will tell everybody else a great story about it. That's the Greater Fool Theory. If they can convince people of the story and get them to buy, then all their clients will get out and they will make money.

One of the biggest losses I ever took occurred because I spoke with a company's management regularly and relied too heavily on what they said. I ignored all market action factors of the stock because management, whom I knew personally, convincingly explained them away.

I bought 100,000 shares of this company at $7. It topped $30, becoming worth more than $3 million. Thus, I enjoyed a very sizable gain of $2 million in the stock.

Then the stock started falling. I kept talking to management and they kept telling me how good things were and not to worry. Each time the stock dropped, they told me that the company was doing fine and that the weakness could not be attributable to fundamentals. They insisted it was just the shorts unjustifiably selling the shares and forcing the price down so people on margin would sell out their shares. They convinced me to stay and hold. Eventually, it went to $20, $10, $1, and then practically zero.

If I had just acted as I normally do—taking a loss after a 15 or 20 percent maximum drop—I would have preserved most of the gain. But instead I let my portfolio decline by $3,000,000—the $700,000 I put up plus the $2,300,000 in forfeited profits. That was one of my worst mistakes. I let a big gain become a significant loss. Although I was a seasoned professional, I suffered precisely because of access to management.

The worst information often comes from management, which either believes or wants you to believe that the company is doing great and that the stock price is cheap and going higher. Management is always biased because it understandably wants its own shares to sell at a high price.

Don't get emotionally involved with management. I can't stress strongly enough how important it is to let the market and price action dictate your behavior. The action of the stock, not the comforting, too often misleading words of management, in most instances tells the real story.

Once in a while you will be wrong pursuing this advice; you will sell and the stock will go much higher. But that is the price you pay for preserving your principal and your gain.

I learned from my bad experience that the best monitoring device for decision making is not what your broker or company management or anybody else is telling you. It is what the stock itself is telling you. That is the best story. If the stock starts moving down, don't listen to the hype and the news. The stock is saying something more important.

A physician I knew bragged that he never took a loss in the market.

"Then what's your problem?" I asked. "Why did you come to see me?"

"For gains," he said.

He put a million dollars into stocks that were selling at substantially lower prices than he paid, which left the total value of his portfolio at $300,000. But he only sold stocks with gains. So he suffered an enormous paper loss and he figured this was a problem. Yet he bragged to me, "I never took a loss." In his mind, he accepted the stocks he owned as being valued at their original cost since he hadn't sold them yet. He just took the view that they would come back.

But the real value of your portfolio is what you can sell it for today, not your cost. Some stocks never come back. Some do. Some go bankrupt. Sitting with losses is certainly the wrong thing to do and taking losses is perhaps the most important discipline you can learn and follow.

Let the price action of the stock dictate your action. If it goes up, add more and pyramid to get rich. If you jumped on a winner, ride it for all it's worth. If it goes down 15 percent from where you bought it or from its high after you achieved a big gain, get out. Don't vacillate—just act.

THE KEY EXCEPTION

There is an important, though rare, exception to this principle and that is when you make up your mind that you've chosen a stock with an exceptional risk-reward ratio that may drop 50 percent or make 2,000 percent. Some stocks are like that and you may want to assume that high level of risk to reward and tough it out. But again, only do it with that portion of your capital that you can afford to risk! If such an exceptional stock hits, it's a home run—maybe a grand slam. If it doesn't hit, you risk some of your capital, but not all of it.

For a wealthy investor, it is an interesting risk. It's hard for some-one with $5 million to find an idea that will really have an effect on their wealth and create a substantial profit—$1 million, $2 million, or more, without ever risking a really significant amount of their accumulated wealth. For a person who doesn't have that much money, it is also an interesting, even an exciting situation, because they are playing for a big score, for an opportunity to dramatically increase their net worth.

So I say: Instead of being in the market and assuming all the risks that the market entails, if you can afford it, take $10,000 or $20,000 and put it into a situation like this, being prepared to lose it all if you are wrong.

If you are right, it could be worth $100,000, $200,000, or more. For someone young, ambitious, and aspiring, or anyone with the guts to go for it, this is the kind of risk to take.

The alternative is taking all of your funds and being in the market all the time, getting an average or slightly better or worse than average return, but never a home run. If you pay $10 and you make 25 percent, you are up to $12.50. But if you make twenty to thirty times your money, as is possible with one of these more speculative stocks, it could mean a real difference in your lifestyle.

If you chance this kind of situation, recognize that you will not sell it at a 10 or 15 percent drop, that you have set your targets, and that you will ride it all the way unless some significant event changes your mind—for example, if it becomes evident that the technology developed by the company you've invested in just doesn't work.

SIGNALS TO SELL

Although no rules fit all situations, it will help you to remember a few guidelines:

- The market action is your best barometer. If the stock is not acting well, if you see a 10 to 15 percent drop, get out without making excuses. Price performance, defined as the stock's behavior, is the ultimate form of communication. The performance of the stock is the best direct communication in terms of picking which ones are winners and which ones are losers. It is communicating its story to you. If you are action-oriented, if you are not paralyzed, then the market gives you the signals.

- If you talk to management, do not rely exclusively on what it says and don't talk to investors who have a bone to pick. The stock is telling you something. Listen to it.

- Write off losses, year-end losses especially, because they are worth money. The government is giving you back part of the loss you take; at the same time, it cleans up your portfolio. I know how hard it is to take losses, but at least the government compensates you with something.

- Sell if the reason you bought the stock is no longer valid; if it doesn't do what it was supposed to do; if the story was wrong; if management disappoints you in any way. Don't rationalize, don't temporize, acknowledge your mistake and wipe it off the books so it stops troubling you.

These points will keep you from falling in love with a stock. Once you own a stock you feel married to it and taking the loss gets you out of that potentially treacherous love relationship. Who knows? That may be a good time to buy, but for you it is really a good time to sell, even though you may be getting an uncomfortably low price and the stock may come back.

The writer of a market letter with whom I worked years ago, a truly brilliant analyst, Walter Gutman, said that different stocks have different personalities, like people.

Certain stocks he could never make money with; they just didn't square with his personality. Others he could always do well with. Some of you may feel that way. No doubt there's a certain stock—or industry—that you feel comfortable with—where you feel you understand its potential and your sense of timing works with it. Other companies or industries baffle you sometimes without your realizing it.

Getting out of a stock lets you look at the situation objectively. If you still like it, you can buy it again; if it turns out to be a loser, you can stay away from it for good. But the crucial factor is that after you take the loss, at least you are no longer wed to the situation and you can make a new decision. You will look at the situation anew rather than just being lethargic and staying with a stock just because you already owned it at a higher price.

To keep your emotions from getting in the way, you may want to enter a stop-loss order. With an over-the-counter stock, which doesn't readily allow you to do this, set a mental stop-loss for yourself and stick to it.

- Unless there's a special reason for you to hold on for another considerable period of time, if your stock advances to a new high and doesn't hold, make the decision to sell if it falls 10 to 15 percent, hard as this is to do on the way down. Just accept less than the maximum profit you could have realized.

- If you jumped on a trend because the stock was doing well and it stops doing that well, sell. Don't ask questions; just get out. If you've been pyramiding a stock and it drops 15 percent, you may lose on your last few buy transactions, but you'll preserve most of your gains.

- Technicians, and sometimes fundamentalists, use market signals to prevent a loss. If your stock doesn't move up while the rest of the market is booming, review your holding. If it's a listed stock and an established company, you may be getting a sell signal.

By the same token, you may want to sell if you see divergences between the Dow and the rest of the market. It's not a strategy I necessarily follow, but it may be an effective way of protecting your investment.

In the end, even the most ardent technician will tell you that your decision to sell must rest on the stock, not the overall market. This is especially true for companies that move in terms of their own life cycle.

A better way is to see whether the market may be so high that certain ratios are out of line. The greatest fundamentalists, such as Benjamin Graham and Warren Buffett, warned investors and stepped out of the way when the market was too euphoric and overpriced and bought when the market was oversold and investors were over-whelmingly bearish. Elaine Garzarelli, the analyst at Lehman Brothers who called the 1987 crash, became famous for being in cash that October. Technical indicators told her—and any number of other investors—that P/Es were too high and dividend yields too low. Unfortunately, many people didn't get out because the market action still seemed too good and because of the prevalent human desire, sometimes called greed, to get the very top. They wanted to squeeze the last drop out of it.

If the market is too high to be a buy, it's a sell, and so is anything that moves with the market. So if you bought because the P/E, dividend, or price/sales ratio was attractive and these conditions changed, you should sell.

The volatility of the markets results in many exceptions to this rule. McDonald's, in the past, dropped sharply from $87 while its fundamentals remained unchanged. However, P/E ratios often do parallel the market. In 1961 the mean P/E on the S&P 500 was 21.68, about as high as it's ever been. In one year it dropped almost 20 percent to 17.39. In 1971 it was 18.50, but it slid to 14.22 by 1973 and dropped still further to 8.94 in the gloomy year of 1974. It didn't really recover for years. Between 1975 and 1979 it dropped from 10.99 to 7.43. The market pulled out of stagnation in the early 1980s and the average P/E rose to 19.27 by 1987.

You would do remarkably well with the patience and the discipline to buy and be fully invested every time the market dropped to a P/E of 11 or less, stay invested through thick and thin until the P/E reaches 20, and then get out, even though big buying opportunities like this don't occur more than once or twice in a generation.

It's not my style. I lack that kind of patience. And, at my age I don't have time to wait for these intermittent broad economic cycles to play out. In fact, it's just too slow for me. I enjoy the excitement and the adventure of the markets and especially discovering and building a big position in an emerging new start-up.

However, when market P/Es reach historic highs, it's a good idea to move to the sidelines or at the very least scale back a little and review your holdings for a sell.

THAT SPECIAL STOCK

What about that special stock, the exception to these rules? The growth company you held for a number of years, through good markets and bad? In this case, your criteria can't be based on the technical action of the market or even of the stock. The time to sell may come when the company is no longer able to respond to change effectively.

A company that was once in the vanguard of change—think of Atari, the first computer game company, in the early 1980s—may find itself obsolete or faced with new competitors because of changing technology. It may be vulnerable to an industry shakeout or an unpredictable event may occur that affects its prospects significantly or permanently. At those times, it's best to stay out of the way, as we did with some of the companies discussed earlier:

- TIE/Communications, at its peak, reached a kind of maturity. It took hold at a time when the telephone industry first broke the AT&T monopoly and for the very first time you could buy and own your own phone. It grew like crazy and its stock price zoomed. Later it became subject to the same intense competition it once presented to AT&T.

- Enzo Biochem also suffered initially as the biotechnology industry moved temporarily out of favor, then as a disagreement with Johnson & Johnson resulted in a long, drawn-out lawsuit. The company is not "mature" yet, with a large number of promising patents and great diagnostic and therapeutic products in development at the same time that it is generating increasing revenues. By any criterion of a growth company, it's still a buy. However, it faces competition that didn't exist before because of the slowness of its expected development and the damage caused by the ambiguities of the lawsuit.

- Genentech stock initially plummeted as sales of tPA (tissue plasminogen activator), a drug which reduces blood clotting, fell below expectations, and the drug's costs raised questions. The stock then became oversold in early 1989 with the price down to the high teens. It recovered when a majority portion of the company was acquired by one of the world's great pharmaceutical companies, Swiss-based Hoffmann-LaRoche. This kind of stock action tells you something about a critical phase of a company's development: At the point when it went into commercialization, when it seemingly should see the sharpest increase in value, it fell apart. Everything it could conceivably do that first year was long anticipated and thus discounted in the stock price. Any adverse news, or rather any achievement—no matter how impressive—that fell short of the loftiest expectations, caused a drastic impact on the shares. In fact, at least temporarily, disappointment with Genentech spread and damaged the whole biotechnology group.

When those stocks first started to drop, long-term holders who were extremely attached to the companies kept envisioning the stocks at their old highs. That is the worst danger, when you don't recognize that you are in turbulent new waters. Industries, like companies, also have life cycles and you can watch mini-industries grow and mature. Federal Express, after years of spectacular performance, slowed its rapid-growth stage. Home Shopping Network, one of the hottest new issues a few years back, fell apart on low earnings and then later made a comeback. Worlds of Wonder, a very hot issue, went bankrupt only a few years after its initial public offering, as the Teddy Ruxpin teddy bear went out of vogue.

One simple and very useful way of assessing a growth company that you've stayed with for many years—through its development phase into commercialization or from zero sales to significant numbers—is to hold it as long as sales, not necessarily profits, keep increasing. Then, sell the first year you see the sales drop. You will cut right through all the detailed fundamental factors otherwise needed to weigh in order to make your decision. The hardest thing is to know when to sell, when to take a profit in order to protect your gains from evaporating into thin air. There is no rule that won't have its exceptions and there is no way of maximizing your rewards and at the same time cutting your risks.

But on the loss side, if you follow the discipline outlined here, at least you can avoid disasters. And if you take the other side of the coin and pyramid winners, you will get rich! If once in your life you happen to get on to a real winner, you will build an important position and achieve magnificent wealth.

End of Chpt. 13

cht. 14
FOURTEEN *goes to pg. 179 = 19 pgs*

INVEST WITH THE BEST: SELECTING A BROKER

A friend of mine invested with a major Wall Street firm that only accepted accounts with a minimum of $250,000. His portfolio did very poorly and his account fell to a pitiful $15,000. He almost lost it all.

To add insult to injury, his broker called him up and said that since his portfolio was now worth so little, the firm could no longer handle his account. He must transfer it out—unless, of course—he sent in enough money to bring the account back up to $250,000.

So if you want to get rich and stay rich in the market, my first prescription is: Work with the best professional you can find. If there's something wrong with your body, you shop around for the best doctors, right? If you want to fight a legal battle that is vital to your existence, you check around for the best lawyer, right? Yet, over many years of experience, I find that people choose brokers carelessly, even recklessly, although their financial existence is as important to them as is their physical health.

Surprisingly, people who learn they carry a fatal disease or that they will be crippled rarely jump out of windows. But because financial success is so exaggerated in our value system, people who lose their fortunes do commit suicide—take a fatal overdose or jump twenty stories to their death. You can tell Wall Street is doing well now because there are more pigeons out on the window ledge than people.

Many people who are brilliant successes may be as miserly as Scrooge. They kept their money under a mattress because they distrust banks and even close associates.

Ironically, these very same people select a broker based upon a hot tip from a stranger at a party or a friend who says, "I just made a killing with this guy, he gave me a terrific stock that went way up." A mere rumor at a social event and they will act on it—or even on a cold call from a firm with no track record.

And, after one fortuitous success, such people will run to the mattress, pull out their money, and throw it all at the broker who gave them that hot tip, greedily thinking, "Why didn't I find out sooner about this easy road to immense riches?" I have seen people do this without making even a minimal effort to find out if their informant or adviser achieved any kind of financial success for himself or his clients.

I know brokers who couldn't pay the rent because they couldn't make a living wage. And these inept people were advising investors with more than a million dollars. Somehow millionaires, who make good decisions when choosing people and making financial decisions for their own businesses, irrationally look to an obviously inferior professional for investment advice: "What should I buy? What should I sell?" Inevitably, they lose money because if the broker doesn't know how to make money for himself and his present client base, he certainly isn't going to make money for anyone else.

I am constantly amazed at how few people check the credentials of brokers. Stockbrokers must be licensed account executives, but registration alone doesn't say anything about them except that they've taken a course and passed an exam on the basics of the stock market, permitting them to get on the phone and sell. A license doesn't equate with talent or even any real qualifications.

Seek out a broker with a track record of personal success investing in the market or one who is affiliated with a firm with a successful track record of performance for its clients.

Unfortunately, many brokers on Wall Street seldom put in real effort. They are lazy. They want to go home at four o'clock. They hang out in bars and get their tips from one another. Usually the person giving the tip has a bone to pick or may even be "stuck" in a particular stock himself. He hopes that by talking it up he can get other brokers to buy it and recommend it to their friends and to their clients. That way the stock might move up and he'll get an opportunity to get out. This, sadly, is too often the attitude and the laziness that persistently prevails in the industry. It accounts for so many of the "hot" stories that constantly make the rounds of boardrooms or the press, which in the end are so rarely borne out. So your choice of broker should not be taken lightly.

If you want to be richer instead of "broker," search out diligently, as if your life depended on it—for after all, your financial existence really does depend on it—the very best and brightest broker you can find to serve you. Only invest with the very best!

ONLY THE BEST

When you invest, realize that you will turn over your most valuable assets—apart from your health and your children—to someone else. Choose someone who cares. Someone who won't forget about you and your account.

Make sure your broker is so interested in retaining your account and making it grow that they will work day and night and weekends and holidays to know the most and be the best; and also that they are dedicated to the proposition that you will be the beneficiary of their prodigious effort.

When you interview brokers, find out if they have been successful themselves! Have they successfully invested for themselves and thus demonstrated an ability to create wealth? You have every right to ask that of a professional before you turn your hard-earned money over to him or her. Usually, good brokers in the process of earning money for their clients will also make money for themselves. So if a broker is financially successful, it is generally a good indication that he is doing well for clients.

Anybody can pick a winner, sometimes. So your questions should be: Has the broker been a winner consistently? Does he or she have a track record? We all have losers. But a broker's performance is measurable, identifiable, just as that of the best doctor. When physicians need an operation for someone in their family, they know the best surgeon to go to or they sure bother to find out.

Be sure that the broker made money by buying stocks for himself or herself as well as for clients. They may be great salespersons or great commission producers or great churners and make a lot of money for themselves, but not by actually investing successfully in the market. Ask directly what stocks they bought for their own account. Ask to see their own personal portfolio and/or track record of performance. Try to get that documented.

Several years ago a self-promoter who once worked for Prudential Bache boasted of an outstanding track record and of having made 40 percent compounded annually on his money. When his story was finally checked, it turned out that he *never* made any money or accumulated *any* significant wealth while he was at Bache. If their records showed anything, Bache said, they showed that he *lost* money. But people, wealthy, accomplished people, too, still believed his undocumented, outrageous cock-and-bull claims that he would return 40 percent annually on their money, and they literally threw their money at him.

Ultimately, he wiped out most of his clients' life savings and produced losses in the tens of millions before his scam was discovered.

It is about brokers like this that clients will brag, "I made a killing on Wall Street. I killed my broker."

CHOOSING A "10"

There are all kinds of people in every field. A brilliant friend of mine once explained to me that only about 10 percent of individuals—including stockbrokers—are "10s" and are at the very top of their profession. These are the real pros. They keep learning long after they are out of school. They are aware of everything. They are brilliant, dedicated, and caring.

At the other extreme are 10 percent who are outright charlatans and crooks—just as there are psychiatrists who mess up their patients by sleeping with them and corrupting their lives. Or doctors who get out of school and never read another textbook, using or abusing their medical degrees by performing risky, unnecessary surgical procedures or prescribing wrong, even dangerous drugs, eager just to generate fees and active turnover to swell their bank accounts.

In between there is a second ranking who are not charlatans or crooks, just totally inept and unintelligent. And then there is a whole range of talent, all the way up the ladder, from poor to mediocre to good to outstanding and finally those 10s who are truly superior and whom you will want to serve your investment needs.

This diversity of ability prevails in every field. Writers who are 10s write brilliantly. They care enough to rework their product again and again until every word is perfect. They know that genius is one percent inspiration and 99 percent perspiration. Then there are writers at the other extreme. They just grind it out and don't give a hoot about the quality of their product, only the hustle and hype it takes to promote it.

In the securities business and in brokerage, you find the same pattern. Only a handful of money managers—the top 10 percent—outperform the stock averages for any length of time, and you must be very lucky to find them. We know who the few outstanding brilliant money makers and money managers are. The middle 80 percent of them are probably just a bit above average, average, or a little below average. They are generally far too diversified to achieve superior results. They don't get paid for making you really rich. They play it safe because they want to keep their jobs and keep making a good income.

At the low end are the remaining 10 percent of brokers who know nothing about their clients, who don't even intend to make them money. All they care about is how fast they can get commissions, how fast they can turn their clients' accounts around.

I have seen great salesmen on Wall Street burn out their clients and say, "There are always new ones." They operate on the assumption that a sucker is born every minute and they can be very successful. They make a fortune for themselves and they keep wiping out their clients.

How these brokers even continue in the business is beyond me. Regulatory authorities, of course, have limited resources, so they cannot follow up on every dangerous broker who consistently damages clients. Unfortunately, these inept, insidious brokers are able to continue in the business. But they are literally destroying people. If they were physicians, they would be killing people, engaged in what could be described as deliberate—not accidental—malpractice.

In other words, these brokers have no interest other than self-interest. They have an exclusively short-term approach. And it is unfortunate but true that many, if not most, people who decide to invest in the market wind up with these brokers, who are often the most aggressive and seductive. They are usually great salesmen. They exaggerate their performance results. They brag. They lie. They hypnotize and inveigle with promises of fabulous results and great wealth. They are convincing because they lack a conscience. They spend no time on research, no time trying to find out about the stock, no time striving to achieve excellence in their profession. They don't even believe in the stocks. Some of them are outright gamblers themselves and actually turn investing into a Las Vegas experience.

Unfortunately, the average investor can't deal with the top 10 percent in this field. The top people are just not available to everyone because they are already overextended.

Accentuate the Positive

The great people are rare. I tell my wife that the secret of my success is like that Johnny Mercer song about accentuating the positive, eliminating the negative, and forgetting about anything in between. I take a group of good people and maximize the positive contributions they can make, minimize the damage they can do, and avoid keeping mediocrity or deadwood around.

It really is a sound method. Even the best baseball team doesn't have all .300 hitters or nine superstars. The shortstop might be a good fielder but has a low batting average. The pitcher can't pitch more than three innings, but he is good at relief. And even a whole team of .300 hitters still won't win pennants if they don't have a good attitude or a good team spirit. So the job is really to put together a team that incorporates, as a whole, the complementary talents and cooperative spirit that make for success.

The key is the leader, but only in part, because other people always make it happen. I'm an assistant to all of my people. I help them make it happen.

I like the advantages of being a small and manageable company. Much as I respect and admire them, I never wanted to be like Merrill Lynch, with hundreds of offices all over the country. I don't like layers of bureaucracy, dispersion, or lack of control. I don't want a lot of offices. We once tried one in California and one in Zurich with only four people, which turned out to be a mistake. It is hard enough to manage people who are close by, with whom you engage in dialogue every day. As every business expands, workers cause problems. To operate at maximum quality and efficiency, you must stay in control.

This is a tough business, a highly regulated and risky business, because we deal with large amounts of money and other people's money. Because it is about money, there are also those brokers— very few—who actually misappropriate clients' funds. For instance, at one brokerage firm, a very solid sales manager took a few hundred thousand dollars out of several accounts. Unbeknownst to his superiors, he was a compulsive gambler and was in debt way over his head. His "creditors" harassed him, threatening that if he didn't come up with the money by Wednesday, they would cut off one finger a day. And then, if he still didn't pay, they would take it out on his children. When you get that kind of threat, there's no limit to what a person will do and he did it. He was trusted because he was with the firm for many years and never did anything wrong before. Sometimes this can be that kind of business.

Some larger firms see these violations and the scary, sometimes enormous losses people bear, as just part of the everyday wear and tear of the business. Part of the risk of doing business in the market is that every year, even every few months, there will be some embezzlement or scandal or loss. Investment advisers expect some bad-apple employees and some level of fraud going on, and also expect to lose a certain number of costly lawsuits.

That position isn't compatible with my personality. It may be true that no matter what precautions you take, there will always be problems and aggravations and lawsuits. But I prefer being small, elite, and manageable in order to minimize the occurrence of these types of problems. I am comfortable with a smaller, leaner dimension and the style it produces, and I feel best off with just one office.

WHO IS IN YOUR CORNER?

Since the best money managers are not accessible to small investors, learn to invest yourself. And if you do it yourself, learn it right by following the approaches mapped out in this book.

If you are a very small investor, the best thing you can do is buy a good mutual fund and let someone who works at it full time manage your money. In this way, you'll be protected from some aggressive, unprincipled, money-chasing charlatan.

Another alternative is finding a talented young man or woman who is up and coming. Someone who doesn't do too much damage—in other words, a 5 or a 6 on a scale of 1 to 10—will put you ahead of the game, if they are honest and caring. At least you are protected from all the 1s and 2s and 3s and 4s, the totally inept or negligent, the promoters and charlatans, the churners who are just interested in commissions. If the broker you choose, whether veteran or newcomer, has genuine concern and potential or finds and follows a good mentor, he or she will do very well by you. Early in my career, I built up accounts that over the years made people of modest means into wealthy people with large accounts. So that is one thing you can do—locate a bright, sincere, dedicated, hard-working up-and-comer.

At the very least, check out the track record of the firm. If you buy from a good firm, you at least have a good shot and some relative safety. Brokerage firms' performances are a matter of public record and anyone who cares to look into them can find out what they are. Yet people often neglect even that minimal amount of homework.

There is no one best way to find a broker. One may be referred to you through a friend or you may find one through an advertisement, through a lecture, or by calling in. Most firms have a "broker of the day" for investors who call in. You're sometimes warned that you're getting a rookie, but it's one way to control the cronyism and abuses that can occur in the highly competitive hunt for clients. You may ask the company's sales manager for a recommendation.

Here are some guidelines that will help you screen your broker and his or her recommendations:

- Think first—don't just jump in with an investment.

- Deal with a firm you know.

- Be skeptical of phone sales.

- Guard against high-pressure sales.

- Beware of promises of quick profits.

- Know the risks.

- Get facts, not tips.

- Ask the phone seller to send you information about the company.

- If you don't understand the material, consult someone who does.

- Give as much thought to investing in stocks as you would to buying a costly piece of property. Indeed, if you don't, it is very likely to be very costly.

IN FROM THE COLD

Be wary of cold calls—that is, when a stranger calls you on the phone, touting a stock or his or her services. This is one of the soundest injunctions around. The fact is, though, that prospecting has become a way of life for brokerage houses, from Merrill Lynch and Smith Barney all the way through the industry. This is not surprising in a society that does more and more business by telephone. Cold calling can be a perfectly good method of getting introduced to a firm. Just check it out, like everything else in life.

Whatever your method of choosing a broker, be sure you screen both the firm and the broker and determine their track record, talent, and honesty. Much will depend on personality. Some people like to be led; others want to be consulted. What is your broker's investment philosophy and approach to doing business? His background and experience? Does he have a college degree or one from a business school? It may be irrelevant to either skill or judgment. But professionals notice a bias toward honesty in higher education that doesn't wear off.

Experience is also important but doesn't necessarily equate to years in the business. For me, the most important factor is having lived through one or two bad markets. Anyone can make money and get clients and referrals in good times. It's the downs that test your mettle—the broker's as much as the investor's. They wash out the drifters, the flashes-in-the-pan, the ones who can't ride it out with their clients or maintain their trust.

See that you share your broker's goals and style. Does he check you out? Does he ask you how much you earn or have in your portfolio and make his recommendations accordingly? Does he ask you to buy on margin? If so, perhaps you are being asked to risk more money than you can afford. Avoid any broker who pulls you into that game.

Does he encourage you to buy options when you know nothing about them and their enormous inherent risk? Many brokers and even brokerage houses love options because the commissions are huge and because their short life span and volatility constantly require you to take action that generates more commissions.

A THROW OF THE DART

With all these horror stories, you may very well be asking: Does it pay at all to have a broker or is it better just to go with a discount house? There's a school of thought, in fact, that will tell you your broker's performance is a function of chance.

In a famous experiment, a number of darts were thrown at a bulletin board studded with the names of companies. The hits were tracked and it turned out that the performance of the stocks chosen at random was better than the performance of the Dow Jones Industrial Average, which in turn consistently outperformed most money managers; on the few occasions when the money managers do better, it's news.

There's good reason not to take all this too literally. Chances are that buyers of the Dow stocks will experience this pattern, largely because the Dow (thirty of the best-known companies) tends to be overbought. But the performance tests also show that the less familiar stocks—the ones not followed by the institutions and the newsletters and dozens of analysts—are more likely to perform better than the favorites. And to find them, you'll need professional help.

Once you're in business with a broker, you can evaluate their professionalism. Do they do their own research and homework? Do they send written material on companies and call periodically—especially if your stocks are down—when so many non-pros go into hiding? Do they return your phone calls? Do they attend to requests that don't generate a commission? Do they ever tell you *not* to buy?

On the other hand, don't expect your broker to call you every other week. If you want to succeed in the market, you must accept a buy-and-hold strategy. Neither you nor your broker can second-guess every swing of a stock. So don't ask where it's going to go tomorrow or next week. If you want to earn the really big returns, the name of the game is patience.

TIME IS MONEY

Watching people's behavior over the years, I sometimes feel they really want to lose.

That sounds funny, but it's true. They use Wall Street and the stock market as they would use Las Vegas. They want the action. They want to "play the market." They're on the phone constantly and it has nothing to do with making money. It may have something to do with turning them on.

But if you want to make money, you don't want your broker on the phone talking to you, calling you and holding your hand, conversing and shooting the breeze with you. Time is money. The broker's time is best spent doing research that makes money for you.

A client once complained to his broker, "I don't like you. I call you five times a day and you don't return all my calls. I only ask for fifteen quotes a day and you don't give them to me. You don't send me enough material. So I don't need your services anymore."

"Gee, I wish I had a hundred clients just like you," said the broker.

"Why?" said the client.

The broker responded, "Because right now I've got a thousand clients just like you."

I observe clients who call up three times a day and ask for twenty-seven quotes. If you have a good broker, what you want him to do is spend his whole day tracking down good ideas, doing research, and finding out about the companies, so that when he makes an investment decision for you, you know it is based on the concentrated investment of time and energy he put in and on the wisdom he is applying. If you need update quotes throughout the day, join America Online or get an Internet account. Then you can watch your stocks to your heart's content.

Why do so many investors use the market like a casino? Doesn't it seem strange? Unfortunately, the reality is that life for most people is boring. They are bored with their jobs and they are frustrated in various aspects of their lives. So they look to Wall Street to turn them on.

One client used to call us on the run from a phone booth because his wife was furious with him. She didn't want him to play the market anymore because he had wiped them out several times already. His boss wouldn't let him play because he had become totally ineffective on his job and was wiping himself out.

This client, a top salesman in the garment industry, became un-

174

productive. He went to the corner, made calls, and prayed. He became a friend after I met him in a tennis league and I really tried
hard to help him make money. The trouble was, the minute a stock
went up one or two points, he would say, "Sell it." Now, if you get
a winner, you must give it a chance to grow; it's hard finding a new
winner every day. But what he really needed was the action, the
excitement, the "high."

That kind of investor turns Wall Street into a race track, but that's
not what Wall Street or sound investing or successful risk taking is
about. You can use it that way, but it's not the way to make money.
And it's even more treacherous if you get lucky once or twice, because then you will believe in that approach.

People don't understand the dynamics of the psychology that
dictates this behavior on their part. Most people can't talk back to
their spouses. They can't talk back to their bosses. They have a
hard time talking back to anybody. So they call up their brokers
and actually hope they will lose money, because then they can rid
themselves of some stress by screaming at the broker. They are delighted to pay for the privilege and don't realize the psychodynamics involved.

Observing thousands of investors and their behavior patterns over
the years, I see that a significant number, if not a preponderance, are
not in the market to make money. In fact, they get frustrated if a
broker makes them some money, because then they can't vent their
spleen, they can't holler at him. So what do they do? They do just
the opposite of what it takes to make money in the market. They
kick out the winners and stick with the losers and do everything
counterproductive to making money.

USE THEIR BRAINS

When I started out as a broker, I told people, "Send me your
money. I will call you, I will advise you, and you act on my decisions.

If I do well, I expect you to give me more money and let the account grow so that both of us can make more and do well. If I don't perform, like the manager of a baseball team that doesn't prove a winner, fire me. Give me the chance to show you what I can do or fire me. I don't want you to abuse me and claim that you can't beat the odds. I'm not your psychiatrist or a way for you to get your kicks." I still believe in that philosophy today.

The way to use a good broker is to let him use his brains maximally and not squander his time on the phone. The people who demand his time may occasionally feel as all gamblers do, that they're going to hit the next Xerox or the next Syntex or the new genetic engineering company that will go from $2 to $200. Yet even if they're somehow, miraculously, lucky enough to find that stock, their broker will have them long out of it by the time it really moves and they are not going to benefit from that big play. Rightfully or not, the fact is that brokers are compensated primarily by commissions and the commissions come from turnover; that is, from buying and, yes, selling. So there is a strong incentive for the broker to turn over accounts. Like it or not, that is one reality we live with.

On the other hand, if brokers care, they will take a longer-term approach. I never cared about the short-term commissions. If I build up a client's account big enough, they'll do very well and eventually I will make a lot of commissions. Not only that, I figured that the more money I made for my clients over the long term, the more appreciative they would be and the more recommendations I would get.

I have fired people who obtained $200,000 from a client to invest and made $100,000 a year in commissions for themselves, while the client got a pile of confirmations and statements from here to the ceiling. The client's accounting bill was bigger than his total profit. At the end of the year, the client would make $5,000 or lose $5,000—perhaps not devastating enough to take away the account, but certainly not good enough to provide a worthwhile return. It was the broker who made the big money. Every time the client made a quarter or a half a point the broker would kick him out of the position and move him into something else. That's counterproductive—a sure formula for losing.

But some people like that because it means they get new confirmations from their brokers every day. The psychodynamics are that people like the sense of activity, the constant involvement, the frenetic communication, the ups and downs and visceral thrills of a Coney Island roller coaster. And they like conversing with their broker, making important decisions. Like the fabulous fantasy of every gambler, they will hit "the big winner" and it will make them rich. And it may, if that one thing happens.

More likely, however, they buy a stock at $2 and when it goes to $3, the broker says, "Let's get out, we have a nice profit; we made 50 percent on our money." And it sounds good. As an inducement to sell, these brokers have an arsenal of clichés and mottoes:

- "Nobody ever went broke taking a profit."

- "You'll cry all the way to the bank."

- "Bulls make money and bears make money but pigs never do."

Nonsense!

As I urged earlier, the smart money doesn't sell the winner. It pyramids it. You can make a killing with an Amgen or a Microsoft or something that comes out at $6 and goes to $100 or $200 and more, as several of our companies have done. If you pyramided TIE/Communications, for example, from $6 to its high of $269, adjusted for splits, you became a millionaire putting your investment in that one company alone. Even if you bought only $6,000 worth in the beginning, never added a penny, and held on to it until you sold it at the high, it would be worth $269,000.

Don't look for action—look for gains. Look for the broker who will help you achieve those fabulous gains.

General Investing Tips

Selecting a good broker is important. Once you pick such a broker you should work with him or her to implement the investment strategies outlined in these pages. Both you *and your broker* should aim to implement the following investment guidelines:

- Stay away from the mainstream. Don't invest in institutional stocks, don't pay any attention to institutional brokers, and don't pay any attention to what the institutions are doing. Find companies that nobody ever heard of and maybe add to those companies that nobody likes.

- Buy stocks. Don't time the market. Just find cheap companies that are good values.

- Buy not only inexpensive companies but emerging companies or early-stage companies, those that others haven't discovered, with outstanding potential for substantial upside reward. This is where you can find some unusual buys, companies with profits and strong balance sheets.

- Be an investor, not a trader. With rare exceptions, nobody makes money trading. Commissions eat you up or you have to pick too many winners.

- Buy small companies. They historically produce the net growth of jobs in the economy. Big companies experience more difficulty moving forward. Small companies prove again and again to be the best place to invest. Recently, they have also given the best rewards and the best risk-to-reward situations.

- Aim high! If you go for the top of the Empire State Building, you may get to the third floor. But if you just go for the third floor, you may never get off the ground. When buying, expect that the stock could be a big, big winner. Otherwise, don't even bother—because the downside risks are there in every stock purchase. You must see the potential reward.

- Look for the best jockeys. I'm excited by the jockeys and their wisdom, their brilliance, their adaptiveness, and their "success neurosis."

- Find companies that grow relatively independently of the economy. Small companies can do that. Large companies are either victimized or rewarded by the total economy, because they are too big to really grow when the economy is down. Small companies can grow even in a down period, because they are just coming on, just making a dent. They can go from a one-half percent share of the market to a one percent share of the market, which can make a magnificent impact on their results. They can double and still grow because they have no foothold. It may be tougher for them, but they can do it. Some companies grow right through recessions. Those are the great ones.

- Concentrate on the companies that Wall Street has not fallen in love with yet, because this is where the opportunities are. Once the investment world falls in love with them, their price goes up and there is no longer much upside. You probably have more risk than reward at this point and certainly not the degree of upside potential or reward that you are looking for.

- Buy creative management, because they are going to make you a winner.

- Don't let any criteria—mine or anyone else's—bind your decision-making process like a straitjacket. Make an exception if you buy the talent of very high quality, very creative management. Never be so in love with a stock that you can't sell it. Keep an open mind. Act, even if sometimes you feel unhappy or unsure of yourself, by selling or buying the stock when you are uncomfortable.

The End of chpt. 14

Chpt. 15 goes to pg. 187=7 pp.

FIFTEEN

THE INSIDER TRACK

There was a man going around town, his mouth open, gasping for breath, and his eyes popping out. So he went to the doctor and the doctor told him he had only three months to live. The man decided, therefore, to spend all his money. He bought everything he could think of.

One day, he walked into a clothing store and said, "Give me a dozen shirts, size 14½ in the neck, 32 in the sleeves."

"Wait a minute," said the salesman. "You better let me measure your neck."

He put a tape measure around the man's neck. "You need a size 16," he said. "If I gave you a 14½ you'd be going around all the time with your mouth open, gasping for breath, and your eyes popping out!"

This story illustrates the importance of the right information in making a good decision. At one time, acquiring the right information—insider information—and then trading off it, was not really a problem.

Trading based on insider information means getting knowledge that nobody else possesses and thus gaining an advantage over people who lack this so-called insider access.

Let's take a hypothetical example.

You just learned that a certain company will be bought out at $60 a share. The company is trading at only $30 a share. You heard about this prospective buyout from some source close to the company. It may be someone in management or the investment banker working the deal. Or someone who works at the company, a broker or lawyer intimately involved with it. It may be a printer with a copy of the documents involved; since code names are used in describing the companies and their products, it's not too hard to decipher them.

A number of people with access to insider information use it before others get in and bid up the price of the stock. You can see it's a sure thing. You can get in early and out fast with a big profit.

If you are part of or have access to this network, you may be tempted to trade on that tip yourself. But don't. This kind of insider trading is a crime.

TAKEN IN

Not too many people remember this, but before 1968, using inside information didn't present much of a problem. Although a law was on the books since 1934, it was practically never enforced and only one important case came to court, *In re Cady, Roberts & Co.* in 1961, which caused little impact on the ways companies gave out their information.

✓ In fact, a Harvard classmate of mine once paid through the nose for what he thought was inside information. He was working for real estate magnate William Zeckendorf soon after leaving school. His secretary's husband was a stockbroker with the highly esteemed firm Lehman Brothers. This broker called my friend constantly, urging him to open an account on the grounds that he would make him rich—despite the relatively paltry sums my friend was then able to invest.

The broker claimed access to all kinds of valuable inside information—groundless rumors, actually—not only because of his connection with the top people at Lehman and its network of private intelligence, but because of his contacts outside that brokerage house.

This broker boasted that he was a member of the FBI before

entering the securities business. Now all his former buddies—both those still in the FBI and those with important positions at major corporations such as Raytheon, General Dynamics, and Martin Marietta—were feeding valuable information into his personal pipeline. "I always know when they're going to get a new contract," he bragged. Years ago, when a military company was awarded a new contract for missiles or aircraft, its stock instantly enjoyed a nice run-up. So what could be better, my classmate friend thought, than getting this supposedly privileged information?

Setting my classmate up, the broker called him regularly and gave him one fabricated inside tip after another. Immediately, my friend called me about the tip and excitedly tried tempting me to share in his imminent good fortune. Once, the broker told my friend that Raytheon would be awarded a major new contract for military microwave communications. My friend bought Raytheon instantly and lost 15 percent of his investment in a matter of weeks. Then the broker told my friend that Eastman Kodak would be awarded a major contract for a camera that could take photographs from aircraft at night. My friend bought Eastman Kodak, and he quickly lost 10 percent on that "hot" tip.

Next came a hot tip on an over-the-counter company that GE was going to take over at a much higher price; Lehman Brothers itself was about to close the deal. That presumably instantaneous marriage never took place, but the broker kept reassuring my friend that it was imminent and persuaded him to stay with it for nine months. Unfortunately, that misadventure cost him more than 30 percent of his investment.

Though these deals never materialized, the broker kept telling my classmate he was just unlucky. He was the only one losing money; all his other clients were making bundles on his invaluable information. "Gee," he said, "I owe you one." He promised to make it up on the next transaction.

It was disarming. How could he leave his broker for another one? Here was someone who "owed" him, whereas a new broker would not be so indebted to him and wouldn't even know him. He stayed with his broker.

Ultimately, this broker wiped out all of my friend's capital, because he urged him to be on maximum margin so that he could make the biggest score on the supposedly priceless inside information this broker was so magnanimously providing him. And when you buy on margin, you can be completely ruined if the stock starts to go down.

I learned a lot from observing that experience.

The broker obviously used the lure of insider information as bait to get accounts and fed his clients nothing but hype. The point is, however, that all these promises or rumors of inside information were being bandied about freely without anyone worrying about going to jail.

Undoubtedly, an important reason why users of inside information weren't prosecuted then was that this information was so ineffectual. Most of it then—just as it is today—was merely rumor or creative salesmanship used by brokers to promote activity or to push up a stock that somebody was already stuck with. Something that any buyer should know—*caveat emptor,* or "buyer beware."

Consequently, so much of this information was spurious that even if someone actually got wind of accurate, useful information at an early stage, no one believed it! People were burned so often by one "sure" inside tip after another that nothing seemed credible.

The Great Scandal

In 1963, however, a company called Texas Gulf Sulphur, listed on the New York Stock Exchange, made a major mining find in a remote place in western Canada. Just about the only ones who could get out there were the geologists working in the field and they used helicopters. As a result, practically nobody knew about the find or its dramatic magnitude, except the geologists and the chairman and president of the company, who went out and aggressively purchased shares for their own personal accounts or for their relatives and friends from then on through April 1964.

Over a two-year period, the stock moved from about $20 to over $100—a truly major move. Many unknowing investors, some of whom had held the stock for many years, saw the shares move up and sold them, right into the hands of those who were in the know— the management and the few friends whom they had tipped.

As the company continued drilling at the end of March 1964, rumors spread in Canada about the amazing find. Then, adding insult to injury, management did something even worse than buying shares on the sly. Hoping to dampen the rumors and the price of the stock, they put out a misleading press release announcing, in effect, that they weren't sure yet what they had found! A few days later they did announce the extraordinary find and the price of the stock soared.

Once the find was disclosed, the SEC looked into the matter and, as the facts unraveled, recognized a clear case of out-and-out highway robbery, of literally stealing from the blind and unaware in the ordinary public. The insiders took advantage of outsiders and traded on their invaluable and closely guarded information. The actions of the top management of Texas Gulf Sulphur Co. seemed so blatant and so obviously unfair to the rest of the public; the SEC took action against them in 1968.

Ever since the *Texas Gulf Sulphur* case, the SEC has cracked down on insider trading with a vengeance, taking on anyone from Merrill Lynch to the tiniest brokerage firms, with ever more cases, broader definitions, and truly substantial fines for flagrant abuse. Ivan Boesky settled for $100 million in fines and penalties plus a jail sentence. Drexel Burnham Lambert paid the SEC $650 million just to avoid going to court.

Today, when you make an earnings announcement, you are required to send it at once to everybody, through a public medium, before you can buy the shares. If your company enjoys a big jump in earnings and you buy stock before the public does, you're considered to be taking advantage of the public, which lacks access to similar knowledge. So you must disseminate that information through the financial wires before you can buy the stock. Even then, you must wait forty-eight hours to do so.

Interestingly, if not for the exposure of the abuse by Texas Gulf Sulphur's management of information accessible only to them, Ivan Boesky and his entire scandalous adventure might never have been prosecuted. Ivan Boesky was wired into a few investment bankers with insider information and some of these bankers actually made a business of selling such information. The ensuing scandals involving Boesky greatly increased the negative connotations and criminal consequences of insider trading.

BE YOUR OWN INSIDER

In fact, inside information was always exaggerated. It was never an effective way of making money in the stock market.

Granted, if you do as Ivan Boesky did—bring $700,000 in a satchel to someone who is already making $2 million a year and yet foolishly wants your cash in exchange for some real inside information—you may make some money.

But this type of activity is truly senseless.

Yes, Ivan Boesky was crazy. He was smart enough, certainly hard-working enough, motivated enough, and dedicated enough, to amass a substantial fortune without pursuing what is so inevitably a self-destructive route.

As a get-rich-quick scheme, inside information is a one-way trip to misfortune. It only lands you in a cell. My conviction is that making a fortune by using your own brains and your own efforts and instincts is much more of a challenge and far more gratifying. You sleep better and reduce your chances of winding up in a jail cell.

Making a fortune legally isn't that hard. Do it by trading on the legal inside information you get by being alert.

Years ago I bought companies that, on the basis of their intrinsic value, seemed promising takeover candidates. I bought Kennecott Copper, Doubleday, RJR, General Foods, Paramount, and a number of other companies that were either taken over or acquired in a leveraged buyout—but I owned them years before the sales occurred.

You do it by spotting value or trends, by looking for companies that are out of favor but may cycle back, or by finding companies that are not yet in favor.

You can find logical, even obvious, takeover candidates yourself. Look for companies that are leaders in their industries, with exciting name brands. When I bought them, the shares of companies like General Foods and Nabisco were selling at prices that didn't reflect either the value of their leadership positions in their industries or even—as in the case of Beatrice Foods or Revlon—the breakup value of their priceless name-brand components.

For those who were wise enough to see the potential of these companies, the opportunities for capital gains were immense. Warren Buffett is perhaps the most universally recognized genius of our time in accumulating intrinsic value.

I like to call this intrinsic value "envisioned value." It means seeing ahead of others, anticipating the ultimate price that, before too long, others will be willing to pay. Buffett proved that this kind of logical, intelligent, somewhat visionary approach works. I believe he made more money in the stock market using this approach than anyone in the modern era.

By now you know that there are many ways to succeed and get rich in the stock market and most of them are legal. But you must pursue your goal with intelligence, total dedication, and a patient and consistent approach.

You must also realize that, as with all successful endeavors, it's hard work. There will be many ups and downs, disappointments and discouragements along the way before you reach the top and achieve the goal you're shooting for.

End of Chpt. 15

SIXTEEN

THE BEST ADVICE IS FREE

A man was lost in the hot broiling desert, his throat was parched, and he was dying of thirst. Finally, to his great relief, he found a woman at the very edge of the desert. Choking and exhausted, he crawled up and asked her where he might find some water to quench his enormous thirst.

The woman replied, "Would you like to buy this tie? For $20 I'll sell you this pretty tie."

The man was in shock. Apparently, he wasn't making himself clear. He tried again to make the woman understand. "Please I'm dying. Where can I get a cup of water?"

Again she replied, "Okay, I'll sell you this nice tie for $15."

"Please, please," he begged. "Water, water!"

"Okay, my last offer," she said, "you can have the tie for $10."

In desperation the thirsty man cried out, "You don't understand. I don't want a tie, just tell me where I can get a cup of water!"

"Okay," she answered, "about a mile down on your left there's a restaurant and you can get water there."

The thirsty man was elated. With new hope, he gathered all his strength and with his lungs full of sand and his throat dry and burning, he crawled to the restaurant. Gasping, on his last breath, he pulled himself up through the front door and grabbed onto the maître d', pleading, "Water, water, please, water!"

"Sorry," said the maître d', "we don't serve anyone here without a tie."

A depressing anecdote perhaps, but it makes a point that you must constantly stay aware of. Always anticipate what is in the offing from what you hear and see.

Be aware of which products and what companies are in demand or will be coming into vogue. This is the key to choosing a stock with enormous potential. The best way to do that is to have inside information.

Did you know you can make money on inside information without risk? It is legitimate inside information and it's all perfectly legal. Whether you're a man or a woman, you can use this inside information to get rich.

One of the best-kept secrets in the business—one that the average security analyst never realizes—is that the best research analyst may be right there in his or her very own home.

It's your significant other—the one who shares your bed and sits across from you at the table for meals and conversation—who often is the best source of investing advice. In particular, because women are often the buyers in our society, I believe they may be the best stock pickers of all.

Statistics indicate that women typically buy most consumer goods—they buy the cosmetics, clothing, home furnishings, drugs, appliances, toys, medical services, gifts, and food. Therefore, they usually are the first ones who discover hot new products and services that hit the market. And they recognize which of these are going to be the winners. Women were the first to snap up Snapple—and it turned into a big winner, quadrupling its initial public offering price within its first year.

Women were the first to know when microwavable popcorn started popping; when Apple home computers first started coming to the home; when the kids started running around in Reebok or Nike sneakers and Gap clothes. That was the time to buy not just the product, but the stock. Any woman who invested when she started using these products made a fortune. And any man who listened made a fortune, too. David Ogilvy, the legendary copywriter, once wrote, "The consumer is not an idiot. She is your wife."

There is a high correlation between the products women buy and the companies whose stocks go through the roof. So if you want to know some inside tips, ask the woman in your life, "What's new? What are you buying?" By being aware of the knowledge available in your own life, realizing what it is that you are intuitively or subconsciously aware of and by applying it to your stock picking, you can make your fortune.

In 1962, I was asked by the New York Stock Exchange to do a series of lectures at business schools, and I gave similar lectures at synagogues and various other organizations. I gave a lecture on this idea of "advice—wives give it free." A few months after a particular lecture I received a thank-you note from a woman who heard me speak. She wrote that because of what I said, she invested in a company which produced a camera she loved using. She said she'd made "quite a nice bundle." She invested in Polaroid.

GET IT OFF YOUR CHEST

Look around your home. Open your medicine chest. When I was a kid, there was castor oil, Ex-Lax, and maybe aspirin—that was it. Today, we stock a dizzying array of drugs, hygienic products, and cosmetics. Where once we bought toothpaste or baking soda, today we buy mouthwashes, plaque looseners, dental floss, Water Piks, and a bewildering variety of toothpastes.

It's a veritable revolution and women are generally first to know about and buy the products that are the basis of our economy. Women are the ones who try the product and repurchase or cross it off their shopping list. Women can explain the advantage of push-up toothpaste dispensers over old-fashioned tubes. They were the ones who liked them and bought them. Women buy the cosmetics and the pharmaceuticals.

Women knew all about Alka-Seltzer—and "what a relief it is." Ultimately, Miles Laboratories, "seeking relief," bought out the company. Neutrogena, the clear soap, was clearly another winner in the consumer market. Minnetonka, a company in Minnesota, developed a liquid soap pump. The stock soared from $2 to $20. Early investors made ten times their money—and because it was a liquid stock, you could have gotten out at any time with a clean profit. Any woman who invested in the stock of these companies when she first started using the product and realized that she liked it, would be rich today for following her own nose.

Women were the first to know about the early pregnancy tests and the birth control pill—home runs for the Searle and Syntex companies, respectively. Any woman who realized what revolutionary products these were identified a big money maker.

How often does a woman go to the kitchen cabinet? Many of the products in those cabinets were great stock buys—Hershey chocolates, Wrigleys, Trident, Sara Lee—all the famous brands. Entenmann's cakes started in a small grocery way back in 1898. Women have been asking for it for nearly a hundred years. General Foods came along and bought the company at a high price with big rewards and big dough for investors.

NutraSweet, G. D. Searle's big winner later acquired by Monsanto, was first tried and used by women. Sweet profits were made on this one. Women also know what breakfast cereals and food products their families prefer: Pillsbury, Quaker Oats, Kellogg's, Campbell's and Nabisco. Nabisco was taken over by R. J. Reynolds. You might have made a fortune in past years by looking in your kitchen cabinet. You still could.

TAKE STOCK OF YOUR SURROUNDINGS

Women know where their families like to eat—McDonald's, Wendy's, or Pizza Hut. Eating out was a lifestyle change that women, when they joined the workforce in great numbers alongside men, initiated and it became part of our way of life. Women brought about this change in behavior—now spreading throughout the world—and of course, they were the first to be aware of it.

When McDonald's was just starting out, Ray Kroc, its founder, owned just one restaurant. He couldn't afford to pay his secretary, so he paid her in stock. For years she was paid in McDonald's stock. She was aware enough to see the potential. Today, she is a multi-millionaire.

When women shopped in the 1980s, many chose Liz Claiborne apparel. When they first discovered they liked this line, they should have invested in the company. Women also started Weight Watchers. It grew into a major company, eventually taken over by H. J. Heinz & Co.

Women often possess the secret of discovering and investing in the winners of tomorrow and it is all legitimate insider trading.

Take stock of your surroundings. Think: What new products did I buy recently that I would buy again? What new products would I love to own? Where am I or my family spending time and money? Then don't just buy the product or service, buy the stock! Remember, if it's hot in your supermarket it will be hot in the stock market.

GOING PLACES

One of the biggest stock winners in the 1990s has been Walt Disney. Parents take kids to Disney World, Disneyland, or Disney movies, watch the Disney Channel on cable TV, and buy Disney videos and Disney licensed products, such as Mickey Mouse watches or Beauty and the Beast hats and T-shirts. And now Disney owns the ABC television network and ESPN. Wow! What a big play that would have been, if only you connected the dots between your real life and Wall Street.

And is there any parent who didn't know about the great prices and fabulous selection at Toys "R" Us? Parents who shopped at Toys "R" Us ten years ago, if they stopped to think about how much they liked it and how popular a place it would become, could have made enough money by investing in the stock to buy all the toys any kid could ever ask for and have lots of money left over for college. How often do you go out and rent a movie? Blockbuster Videos was a blockbuster idea and one terrific growth stock for many years.

Women loved The Limited. The owner of Limited Stores is a leader in growing department stores. The company now has more than 5,600 stores. Currently operating Limited Stores, Henri Bendel, Limited Express, Victoria's Secret, Abercrombie & Fitch, Structure, Bath & Body Works, and Limited Too among others, there seems no limit to the expansion and growth of this chain. If you bought Wal-Mart shares because it was your family's store of choice, you latched on to one of the greatest all-time stock market winners.

Where do you stay when you vacation? See the potential of new places as well as new stores and products.

BUY WHAT YOU KNOW

When you see someone you know buying a product or patronizing a place, find out if the company is public. If it is, buy it. And buy it early. You need not be a genius. Just be in touch with the world around you.

Years ago, housewives were first to see the advantage of fluorescent lighting and Formica. More recently, it's cellular car phones, the second generation, which are showing up in women's cars as well as men's. Be smart: Don't just buy the phone. Use it to call your broker and buy shares in the new cellular companies.

Women are the first to recognize many trends in entertainment technology.

Is there a bigger entertainment growth industry than cable TV? Women made the Home Shopping Network an overwhelming success. Home Shopping Network stock came out in 1986 and went to more than $130 in less than five months. If you were tuned in, you saw your stocks in this emergent company rise meteorically.

My point is this: Buy the companies you know and love.

Women are also aware of what their husbands and boyfriends are buying. The do-it-yourself market exploded in recent years. We now have large warehouses where we can shop for all our home improvements. Home Depot is a leader, especially in the Midwest, Southwest, and California, where people do more of their own home fixing. It is the new place to shop and one of the top winners of the last decade. Had you invested in this one you would have "built" your fortune.

Look at which car the man in your life is suddenly saving up to buy. Let him buy the car. You buy the stock and ride a winner. Years ago, Jaguar became especially successful because women liked it and drove the stock way up.

Rx FOR SUCCESS

In 1986, with concern about AIDS mounting, condom use became more widespread. Carter Wallace, the nation's leading condom manufacturer, controls 55 percent of the market. In 1986–87, its stock went from about $48 to $150.

Contact lenses—hard, soft, colored—are another wonderful medicine-related growth business.

If your doctor says, "This is something we now prescribe to thin the blood and prevent heart attacks," you not only learned about new drugs, you've stumbled onto a new investment opportunity. You may learn Prozac is being prescribed a lot. Buy the company that makes it. Roche Laboratories markets Valium and Librium. Merck consistently broke new stock price highs with new drugs such as Vasotec and Pepcid, which are used in cardiovascular and anti-ulcer therapy, or Mevacor, which reduces cholesterol, or Proscar, which brings down the size of enlarged prostates. You get the picture—Merck is a leader in bringing out exciting new health-enhancing products. Its shares will likely enhance your wealth.

Everyone you know is potentially a good lead as to what is being prescribed generally. New drugs or medical technology may be winners in the stock market. That is why medical and biotechnology companies are so promising and offer such outstanding rewards.

In matters of office technology, secretaries were the first ones to use and appreciate word processors, which were developed for the office of the future. If you invested in Wang word processors when they first appeared, you would have had the last word on getting rich. Since then, other companies made Wang obsolete—I learned *that* from my secretary, too. She knew Apple and Compaq were newer and better and that Microsoft provided software that was easier and more productive. If only I had asked her, I would have had a big position in these super growth situations early on.

Not so many years ago, every time you wanted a copy you put blue carbon paper in your typewriter. The carbon copy business no longer exists, replaced as it was by photocopy machines. If only more secretaries had invested in Xerox at the time of that quiet revolution, more bosses might be working for them!!!

BE IN TOUCH WITH BUYING BEHAVIOR

You need not hold a stock forever. When you see a product catching on, buy the stock. When you feel it is in decline, sell it. The Barbie doll was a hot product when it first came out. Its popularity leveled off or even declined for a time, but now it's catching on again.

Study your daily routine. Are you suddenly using the fax machine or Federal Express instead of the mailbox? Do you bring movies home instead of going out to the neighborhood cineplex? Do you answer your own phone or is a machine doing your talking?

I listen to my wife.

She once advised me to buy diamonds.

I said, "What if they don't go up?"

She said, "Then I'll keep them."

Our company is successful because we pick up on new trends and underwrite companies in these areas.

The emergence of many of our companies coincided with cultural revolutions, social and behavioral changes that were taking place. Investment success comes from timing new products with new needs.

End of chpt. 16

SEVENTEEN

chpt. 17 *goes to pg. 203=5 pgs.*

UP YOUR PORTFOLIO

To succeed in life you must clearly define your goals, know exactly what it is you hope to accomplish, and then conceive of a plan or strategy. Only then can you achieve these goals.

The same holds at least equally true in the stock market. You need a plan in order to "up your portfolio."

There are many ways to get rich, and people become rich in different ways, but almost everyone who accumulates great wealth follows a consistent plan. In other words, don't do one thing one day and the entirely opposite thing the next. Don't be a trader today and a long-term investor tomorrow. You can't buy fad stocks one day and hot tips the next day. Determine the direction you are headed and which of the previously outlined strategies you will adopt. By all means, be innovative, but stay on track.

APPRECIATING APPRECIATION

Another important rule is: Seek capital gains rather than dividends, no matter how appealing the yield may look. Buy stocks for appreciation. (If a stock you like pays good dividends, that is another matter.) In other words, if dividends are included in that appreciation, great! You've got a bonus. But don't feel secure just because you are getting a dividend. In four declines in a stock's price on a single day, you can lose more than an entire year's dividends. In an hour, stocks sometimes move up and down more than their dividends might total in two or three years.

Don't buy for dividends! Warren Buffett, the smartest investor, pays no dividends. He reinvests the money and compounds it. That's why the stock of his company, Berkshire Hathaway, is one of the biggest winners of all time, rising from $38 a share to an unimaginable $48,600 a share over the last two decades.

The smartest investors don't want dividends on which they must pay a tax. They would rather have the management, providing it's a growth company that knows how to make money on its money, reinvest it in the business, and thereby enhance the value of the shares, providing maximum capital appreciation in the stock price for its investors.

As for straight preferred stocks or straight bonds, avoid them or buy them only for temporary periodic diversification and generally not for any long period of time. They are inevitably ruined by inflation and by consequent fluctuations in interest rates.

Don't go for fads. Try, instead, to identify a company that is in a new, emerging industry. It is a fad if you buy into a Hula Hoop company that benefits from a temporary, fleeting vogue. It is not chasing a fad to find a biotech or pharmaceutical company in which you see a new, uniquely outstanding opportunity.

I would also advise—as a matter of fact, I'd make it a hard and fast rule—avoiding penny stocks or "Denver" stocks, as they're sometimes called. These are the very cheap stocks that are often issued for a penny or a nickel a share out of brokerage houses usually located in Colorado and Utah. Unfortunately, far too many people do not realize that even though these stocks sell for pennies, they may be overpriced relative to their earnings or performance. They say, "Wow, if my million shares at a penny go to only a dollar a share, from a $10,000 investment I'll make a million dollars."

It sounds like a good shot and people love that. But to reach a dollar from a penny, the stock must move up a hundred times and it's not likely to do that. The fact that a stock costs only a penny means nothing, because there may be 900 million shares outstanding. At a penny a share, the company would be valued at $9 million. Yet the entire company, all of the shares together, might not be worth even $1 million.

The people who issue these securities are looking for gullible victims. They are exploiting naïve investors with no knowledge of the market who think that by paying only one penny a share they are getting a bargain. These investors don't realize that by any professional measure, based on the total number of shares outstanding, the company may have an extravagantly high valuation in relation to its future opportunities, its proven achievements, or its net worth. I never met a truly smart money professional willing to touch these stocks. The people who make a fortune on them are the often fly-by-night issuers and the brokers who sell them, not their public clients.

But some people take the attitude that "Well, it's only a penny or two cents. How much can it go down? How much can I lose?" Well, you can and probably will lose your entire investment. If you bought 1,000,000 shares at a penny a share, that's still $10,000— probably 10,000 hard-earned dollars too.

As with everything else, there is an occasional penny or Denver stock—and I mean very occasional because you probably have better odds in your state lottery—that went from a penny to 65 cents. But for the rare $5 million or $10 million made in that one issue, there is probably a billion dollars lost collectively in all the other issues.

So as a rule, I say: Stay away from penny stocks. In 99.9 percent of the cases you'll save yourself money and aggravation and if you follow only this one piece of advice, this book will be just about the best investment you ever made.

NOTHING IS GIVEN MORE LAVISHLY THAN ADVICE

In my opinion, you are unlikely to get rich by consulting your banker, your lawyer, or your accountant. Don't take the advice of an expert whose expertise is not the market. They may protect you against your worst blunders, which for many people is perfectly valid and important counsel, but they are not stock pickers. They may be experts in their own field, but very few lawyers, bankers, or accountants ever became rich because of stocks they chose themselves, independent of a good broker.

You shouldn't let your banker do your accounting, you shouldn't let your stockbroker prosecute your case, and you shouldn't let your lawyer pick your stocks. An expert on stocks is the one to turn to for expert advice on investing. Consult the best, most highly recommended broker you can find.

If you decide to choose your investments yourself, be aware. Don't underestimate the time and energy you must devote. No one can command their investments by devoting only a few hours a week to them. Even a serious investor, monitoring the market, can scarcely give their portfolio all the attention it needs.

And don't depend on luck. In the market, luck is a function of dedicated diligence and hard work. The harder you work, the luckier you'll get.

True, the stock market is more an art than an exact science. And some investors, like great artists, are blessed with innate ability. Yet even the most brilliant artists must work with enormous dedication, putting in long hours over an extended period of time.

No matter how gifted you may be, to compete for wealth and success in the market, you will need to sweat to perfect your skills, excel in your results, and reach your peak.

GAMES PEOPLE PLAY

Above all, don't crapshoot. Don't generate activity just for the sake of activity. Don't short-term trade in and out. Many people feel compelled to be active in the market and they do day trades for the excitement. No one to my knowledge ever got rich day trading. Even the traders on the floors of the exchange, who are right there and pay no commissions, don't get rich day trading.

The trouble is, many people are in the market for fun—for the ups and downs, the thrills and spills. They play the market. Why even call it play? The market is not a game. It is your financial life. People use the market for excitement, as if it were a horse race, but remember: You play the horses. You don't play the market. The market is the place where you invest or speculate—where if you develop a consistent discipline and use your brains you can be a big winner.

It can only be naïve stupidity or laziness that makes people think that investing is different from any other situation requiring expert professionals. It is the Las Vegas approach, the one where you roll the dice and hope to G-d you get lucky. It shouldn't be that way. The market is not Las Vegas. It is not a "random walk" either, and it is not based on chance.

In Las Vegas, with rare exceptions, only the house makes money. In the market, by contrast, everyone can make money, because there are growing businesses, rising markets, and opportunity. But it's not a matter of luck; you don't just get lucky. The irony is that if you take the Las Vegas approach and somehow get lucky once or twice, you are worse off. Because then you become reckless, forget the risk, and blow everything you've gained and a lot more.

Study and master the art of the market and you will get richer than you ever dreamed.

End of chpt 17

(Last chpt.) chpt. 18 goes to pg. 218 = 14 pgs

EIGHTEEN

THE CLOSING BELL

I don't believe in "market timing."

A nice old plumber once came to fix our sink. He was working under the sink with the drainpipe opened when my wife asked him if he'd like a cup of coffee. He said, "No." She said, "Are you sure? I already made it." He again said, "No, thank you." So she poured it down the sink. The coffee went down the open drainpipe right into his face.

What is coming to you in life is coming to you—one way or another. If things are going to go up, they'll go up. If they're going to go down, they'll go down.

I really have no idea how to predict the market. I don't know what the market is going to do in the next hour or the next day, much less in the next three days or three months. I don't think anyone has the capacity or genius to identify every upswing and downswing.

Some technicians say, "We're going to have a bull market for another three months. It will move up for the next three months and then down by the end of the year." Or they'll say, "I like the market. By the end of the year, I think it's going to be higher, but during the next ninety days it will be lower."

I preface my forecasts with this quote that appeared in a leading daily financial newspaper. It is from a Boston University energy expert who said: "Oil prices will go up or down, more or less, unless there are some unforeseen circumstances."

Technicians follow the endless fluctuations of the market and tell you to trade in and then trade out. They pretend to divine it all. They make predictions, not because they really know, but because they are asked to and because that's what they get paid to do.

My friend Louis Rukeyser, the well-known financial commentator and brilliant moderator of the television program *Wall Street Week,* once noted that "Technicians are like generals—always fighting the last war."

Technical market analysts, he said, are marvelously interesting people, taking chart wiggles and graph squiggles and assorted other forms of alchemy and then telling you what absolutely, positively must happen next to common stocks. In the short run, as in the case of zillions of monkeys pecking at typewriters, one of them just might come out with Shakespeare. In the long run, though, a used Ouija board will probably serve you just as well.

The most useful technicians are those who don't pretend to be flawless gurus, but just try to give you some continuing sense of the market internals. Remember that the technicians tend to base their forecasts on what occurred in the past and remember that human beings in the real world are funny and unpredictable things. Which is kind of nice.

Few technicians possess good records of crystal ball reading, in retrospect. But thousands do it, anyway, and you will inevitably find a few who are right. Even a broken clock is right twice a day so the saying goes; but it seems to me it is mostly an accidental and rare occurrence.

When people talk about market timing, they usually mean buying and trading, getting in for a few days and getting out. Some exceptional pros do that, but I know few who get rich at it.

STIMULATING ACTIVITIES

The contribution that technicians make is largely descriptive. In effect, if the market is going up, then it is going up. If the Dow breaks out through 10,000 on the upside, then it is going higher. If the Dow dips below 10,000, it is going lower. That is a tautology; it is not a prediction.

If you listen carefully, you will detect another rationale or better still, another underlying motive. You will find that technicians are really trying to stimulate activity and thus generate more commissions, which is why brokerage firms love them.

Technicians stimulate activity by telling you what is going to happen today and tomorrow, this afternoon and next month, and by causing people to make buy and sell decisions on the basis of their predictions.

There are a great deal of commissions generated and money made by technical analysts who tell you that you should sell your positions or that you should buy new positions because they don't like the technical action of the stock you own. Much the same is true of program trading—the computerized selling that you get with institutions.

When I worked at Shields, a very bright technical analyst generated a great deal of business for the firm, but he himself never became rich. I've never met a rich technician. If there are any rich technicians, it is because they make good money selling their services. *Not* because they made good money in the market for themselves.

Technical analysis may be useful as one instrument within the entire array of approaches to the market, but in some respects, it is sometimes self-fulfilling. If enough technicians make predictions and they all make a given prediction at once, the cumulative effect can be a self-fulfilling prophecy.

Most of what happens in the market that instigates the major moves is generally unexpected. It is unexpected because presumably everything that is known is already digested and reflected in the market—that is, discounted—at all times.

SOME SAY UP, SOME SAY DOWN

I've always felt that the market is far more amenable to psychoanalysis than to security analysis. Just to prove it: Almost every day in the newspapers you will find as many so-called wise, sophisticated professionals telling you why it will go down as there are telling you why it will go up.

A professor at the Harvard Business School taught me the best lesson ever on statistical probabilities. Every year, he asked his entire investment management class of two hundred outstanding students to predict where the Dow Jones average would be a year out. Then he took all of the students' answers and plotted them on a chart. Every year, the answers turned out to form a bell-shaped curve—a random distribution. And the amazing thing was that in every single one of his classes, without exception, ever since he began teaching at Harvard Business School perhaps twenty-five years before—it was always a bell-shaped curve! Every single course, every year, it came out the same.

Everybody predicts. The majority will predict that the market will be selling right around where it is because that is where it is safe. So, if the averages are 8,000, most people will predict that the low will be 7,000 and the high will be 9,000.

Then you get the deviants: a few people who are a little more bearish and more pessimistic; or more optimistic. The pessimist thinks that the world will end or that the banks will go bankrupt and that the averages will drop to half their present level. The optimists predict that the average, which is now 8,000, will rise 50 percent, to 12,000. The way-out maniacs say it will be 15,000.

All this conjecture really has nothing to do with the stock market. It is a function of the predictors' personal outlook and behavior, their view of the world. Predictions are thus no more than a mirror of human nature.

Predictions are just meat for the media to gnaw on. Reporters call me up and say, "What do you think?" And then they call up somebody else. They will call around and every day they'll find a new reason, no matter how far out, for these fluctuations. The news media must fill up their newspapers and the six o'clock news, so they always call brokers and research people and they always get a story.

THE PENDULUM SWINGS

There is a broader sense to market timing that anybody can use. These are the real signals or signposts, of major change—so-called sea changes in the market.

Wall Street is like a pendulum, exaggerated at both extremes. There are times when stocks are in vogue and there are times when they are out of vogue. When people are enthusiastic about stocks and the economy, when they feel good about the world and the political situation, they become enthusiastic about the future and run stocks way up beyond what they are worth.

At the other end of the pendulum's swing, everyone is down, depressed. During Jimmy Carter's presidency, for instance, the political feeling was negative; people felt he was wishy-washy and exhibited a poor sense of leadership. Accordingly, the overall market stayed depressed or performed poorly.

Of course, real factors do affect the market—the earnings outlook, inflation, the U.S. federal budget, trade deficits, and interest rates. But you'll find as often as not that the market refuses to respond to the factors it says it's responding to because it already discounted them. Or else it reacts in wild exaggeration, all out of proportion to the events that triggered the move.

Wall Street is that kind of community and you must identify which phase it's in. Wall Street swings between extremes of fear and greed. When people are excited and it's a bull market, they pay for what I call *Olam Habah,* which in Hebrew means the world to come—the hereafter. Determined to discount all of the glowing promises of eternity, they pay now for all future dreams.

In periods like these, as in the euphoric bull markets of the late 1960s, the future is discounted very rapidly. In the 1960s, people said, "This company just got a contract from IBM. In three years, it's going to have five dollars in earnings per share. If you pencil in that growth, that stock should have a value of a hundred dollars a share." If the stock were selling at only $4 it would promptly go crazy, shooting up like a rocket—sometimes moving up as much as $5 a day or more. While it lasted this kind of move was great, but once reality set in, as it inevitably did, the illusion withered, so too did your hard-earned money as the stock price plunged.

Years ago, there was excitement about Polaroid and its phenomenal growth—the marvelous new company with the new instant camera. Forecasters on the Street projected what Polaroid would do and insisted that you should buy it at $200 a share because in five years, at the rate it was growing, it would be worth $6,000 a share or thereabouts. Then one day, a wise research analyst named Walter Gutman, with the incisive precision of a skilled surgeon, calmly punctured that balloon, at least for me. He said, "If you accept the logic of this extrapolation being done by the analysts on the Street, then at the rate they are projecting Polaroid's revenue growth, in nine years Polaroid will be larger than the GNP. Everyone chuckled, realizing it was preposterous. And eventually the stock came back down to earth, too. But, of course, when you take a big compounded growth rate and extrapolate it several years into the future, as analysts often like to do in bull markets, then you know the stock price predictions are going to get very overblown.

PSYCHOANALYSIS VS. SECURITY ANALYSIS

That is why markets are more susceptible to psychoanalysis than to security analysis: because investors suffer mass hysteria. When they're bullish, they pay exorbitantly for their dreams. They pay for what they think the stock will be worth five years down the road. Investors put a number on their dreams and pay for the entire next world. They pay for eternity and then discount it to the present. Sometimes, they don't even discount it to the present. They are rewarded accordingly.

Often you can get rich in the market just by following the trend. In a bull market, you'll find many opportunities like that. The most money is made when everybody is bullish and everyone is paying today for the distant future. Of course, the biggest risk exists at that time, too, but nobody wants to get out. It's too much fun. It's too easy. The gains seem there for the taking—so why hesitate? Throw caution, common sense, and logic to the wind—join the party and the fun. Everyone is greedy.

When the market is bearish or when the mood is pessimistic, the very same companies may not present much different earnings, but investors don't even consider the present, much less factor in the potential for the future. Sometimes the companies will sell for less than even their cash value, not to mention their book value or net assets.

Nobody really knows when the market will go sour—nobody could have predicted either the bull market during 1987 or the devastating crash that smashed it down 23 percent on October 19 of that same year. Every day the financial media tell you what is going up and what is going down. Rarely do they predict the bear markets. And the major moves, no one consistently predicts. They happen and it is largely a matter of crowd psychology that everybody suddenly picks up on at that particular time. Suddenly, a major run up—a bull market—can come about. Because of the tax laws, the optimistic mood, the positive political climate, or just the fact that everything else is up.

THE TAIL OF THE BULL

The end of a bull market is generally identifiable by the fact that all the speculative stocks start moving, including what used to be referred to as the "Denver junk" and the penny stocks.

They suddenly—and rather often—invade the most active lists. You see big premium openings on initial public offerings—high premiums on stocks being offered at unbelievably and unsustainably huge multiples of their earnings to start. In other words, they command a very high valuation, yet they still go up at the opening. You see the irrationality and emotion dictating the pipe dream. The Greater Fool Theory is then in full gear. There are instant rewards. Everyone is doing well—just as in 1929, when even the shoeshine boy made money in the stock market.

In 1969, for example, when we brought out a new issue at $5, it would open at $15, even if it was just a start-up. We had no problem selling it. The demand was overwhelming for every new issue.

When that happens, it's great fun.

Everybody makes money quickly and we all feel like geniuses. But it's really the last stage. The stage when everybody is throwing his money into the market without figuring out values or even bothering to do research. They're just factoring in every good thing that might happen to the company over the next generation.

That is the signal that the end of the bull market is near. Because it isn't really all that easy to make money. Yet everyone is doing it. It may be hard to get out in the middle of all the euphoria, but the elation, more than anything else, is the surest sign that it's all over.

The end of a bull market may also be heralded by some prominent and conservative investor suddenly, belatedly, becoming involved. This happened at the end of the bull market in 1972 in low-priced and speculative stocks. The head of an Ivy League university made a statement that the university should be more aggressive in its investment approach and participate in this segment of the market.

By the time the conservatives say they ought to be in the speculative segment of the market because their returns aren't high enough—as high as the market has recently afforded—that is the end of the bull market. And in fact it was. The Ivy League university put some money into highly speculative situations at the height of the market and was badly hurt.

When brokers are hiring drivers and buying yachts, that's when you can be sure the end is near.

Other, less anecdotal indicators can also pinpoint the high of the market.

The Dow may be out of sync with the overall market. It keeps going up and up and up, but other issues don't follow. More stocks will go down than up, so the advance/decline line becomes weak even as the Dow reaches new highs. The volume for advancing stocks won't be in proportion to the number of stocks that are advancing. Or the daily most-active list will show more down stocks than up stocks at the close.

The Dow theorists will tell you that if the Dow Industrials are not backed by the Dow Transportation Index, moving in the same direction to confirm the trend—then it is signaling that the trend is over. Or they will tell you that if the Dow Jones Utilities don't follow the Industrials, you're not getting a strong signal.

Stocks may be drifting down on low volume. When that happens, investors who were selling into strength can produce an avalanche if they find that buying has dried up.

Unfortunately, in most cases you only see the total picture in retrospect. There were three predictors of the severe market downturn in November 1971, but they occurred over a period of a year, in May 1971, in June 1971, and in July–August 1971. And they were broken by buy signals.

Fundamentalists are adamantly set against market timing, but they can also tell you when the market is overbought. Historically, at two times book value, the Dow is considered expensive, as is the Dow's dividend yield when it falls below 3 percent. The Dow is considered overpriced when it reaches eighteen to twenty times earnings, approaching the P/Es of growth stocks. These indicators may not be absolutely predictive, but they do send a message: Speculation may be getting out of hand.

In the spring of 1987, we seemed near the end of a bull cycle. When people asked me about it at that juncture, I'd say, "We seem to be almost at that point, but not yet. Not to the same degree, compared with other periods." The indicators weren't all in place. It was a bull market in blue chips. Everyone rationalized the prevailing high prices by arguing that they were cheap by Japanese standards! Most people hadn't yet noticed that Japan's market was in the midst of its own insanely overpriced bubble, one created by systemic fraud. If the American market was at a much lower P/E ratio than the Japanese, it was rationalized, then it must still have a long way up to go. The Japanese market then proceeded to drop from a high of 40,000 to less than 16,000, or more than 60 percent, before bottoming out in 1992. We really could have, indeed should have, seen it coming, because the over-the-counter market, an indicator of speculative activity, hadn't moved significantly as a whole for four years. But caught as we were in the existing euphoria, the precipitous drop caught many of us unawares.

The hypnotic, all-encompassing effect of periodic, recurring mass euphoria, in which prices go up to what are in retrospect unimaginable heights, is nowhere better captured than in Charles Mackay's nineteenth-century classic, *Extraordinary Popular Delusions and the Madness of Crowds*. This book describes such mass phenomena as the tulip craze and the Mississippi land rush, in which seemingly normal, rational people paid the most ridiculous prices for these so-called investments that they were rushing to buy in the sheer expectation of quickly selling it to another eager buyer at a much higher price. To give you a historic frame of reference and as a means of understanding the markets, read this incisive treatise. It illustrates just how difficult it is to get out at or near the top—when everyone is cleaning up and is absolutely positive that things will go much higher—and why it is so urgent that you do get out, before you get wiped out.

It's great to be in a bull market and share its spectacular rewards. But when the raging bull begins to roar too much—get out of its way!

THE BEAR FACTS

The reverse, a bear market, is marked by almost exactly the opposite signs. A bear market is signified by everybody being nervous and dumping stocks, again to the point of irrationality. You get emotional selling. People look at the values out there and say, "The balance sheet, the liquidation value of the company is a dollar and I can't even sell it for 80 cents." Then they get nervous and try to bail out.

We've seen several cycles of euphoria and gloom since World War II: great bull markets in 1950–51; the go-go years of the 1960s; the bull market in 1971–72; a long period of sustained growth between 1982 and October 1987; and most recently, the bull market stampede that began accelerating in January 1995.

They were interrupted by severe bear markets in 1957–58, 1962, 1966, 1969–70, 1973–74, 1978–81, and October 1987–88.

When everyone is bearish and even the pros are pessimistic and unwilling to invest, when everyone is moving toward liquidity, saying, "I just want my money in the bank. I want Treasury bills," that is the best opportunity to buy stock cheaply. And that is why "contrarian" psychology—doing the opposite of what everyone else is doing in the market—works.

When everybody is bearish, that's the opportunity to buy. When everybody is bullish, usually no one has any liquidity. They already invested all their money. They cast their votes and used up their dollars—because in the market you vote with your dollars. They are at the end of the cycle. Everyone is fully invested and there is no one left to buy your stock.

Whereas in a good market optimistic investors pay for fanciful dreams of the future, when the market goes bad they often aren't willing even to pay for the cash just sitting there in the company. In such an environment rare opportunities do, nevertheless, exist. Amazingly, you can sometimes buy companies in a recession at less than their "under the hammer" liquidating price. You can then, often, buy them for less than two thirds of hard, real book value— and even for less than their working capital or net current assets.

Again, you must be aware that this is a time when you will be the most anxious, the most fearful and any action will seem the riskiest. But when it looks like the world is coming to an end, that is your opportunity to make some really big money.

YOU CAN DO IT TOO!

You have now been introduced to the best investing advice and strategies I have discovered and developed. It is now time for you to take action! Trust me! Believe me! You can succeed if you apply the lessons I have shared with you in this book. Don't be afraid to bet on yourself. You are now fully armed and equipped to make a fortune.

Just as I have encouraged you, the reader, to follow the advice and guidance discussed in this book, I have also tried to encourage others, many of whom have worked for me at one time, to take action and go out on their own. I think their stories are truly inspirational.

Kevin Kimberlin, for example, was one of Blair's most successful investment bankers. In 1986, while working for me at Blair, Kevin helped found The Immune Response Corporation, which I described earlier in this book, and recruited Dr. Jonas Salk, the creator of the polio vaccine, to the company. Today, Immune Response is a publicly traded company with a market capitalization of over $250 million. Kevin then left Blair to join Spencer Trask Securities as head of its investment banking division.

Among Spencer Trask's many successes since Kevin joined the firm was its early stage investment of $1.5 million in multiplexing fiber-optic technology (which greatly increases the transmission capacity of optical fiber). Remarkably, this initial investment of $1.5 million grew in value to $250 million in less than five years. The multiplexing fiber-optic technology became the platform for the establishment of Ciena Corp., which in its IPO in February 1997, underwritten by Goldman Sachs, raised $115 million, and in a subsequent offering in July 1997, also underwritten by Goldman Sachs, raised an additional $400 million. Ciena continues to grow at a dramatic rate.

Wally Steinberg came to Blair from Johnson & Johnson where he had spent twenty-one years and had been responsible for the creation of numerous innovative products, including the "Reach" toothbrush, which became a phenomenal hit. Wally worked for me as an investment banker, and then left to form Healthcare Investment Corporation, which grew into the largest venture capital fund devoted exclusively to health care. Through Healthcare Investment, Wally financed many pioneering companies in the health care area.

Today, for instance, Human Genome Sciences, a company that Wally founded through Healthcare Investment, is a leader in the growing field of genomics (discovering genes that can be used as the bases for new medical treatments). Human Genome Sciences is a publicly traded company and has a market capitalization of close to $1 billion. Another of Wally's big successes is MedImmune, Inc., which he also founded through Healthcare Investment. MedImmune is a pioneer in developing products for infectious diseases and transplantation medicine, and has several promising new drugs in clinical trials. MedImmune is a publicly traded company and has a market capitalization of approximately $800 million.

One last example is Dr. Marlene Krauss, an <u>ophthalmologist</u> who also worked at Blair as an investment banker. While at Blair, Marlene helped launch Summit Technologies, a developer and manufacturer of ophthalmic laser systems designed to correct common vision disorders. Summit has been successful, selling its lasers in over fifty countries. Marlene later left Blair to become one of the founders of KBL Healthcare Investment Banking, another leading venture capital firm in the health care area.

Interestingly, Marlene came to Blair in 1965 after graduating from the very first Harvard Business School class that included women. She worked for me initially for seven years as an investment banker and did an outstanding job. At the time she was also a leading advocate for women's rights and achieved enormous media recognition for her work at Blair in what was then a field heavily dominated by men. While at Blair, Marlene started taking courses at Columbia Medical School, where she developed a strong interest in ophthalmology. She applied to, and was accepted at, Harvard Medical School, and I encouraged her to return to school to pursue her growing interest in medicine. Not surprisingly, Marlene became a world-renowned ophthalmologist. After several years of practicing medicine, Marlene asked me if she could come back to Blair because she had concluded that her most fulfilling professional experience was as an investment banker. I was, of course, delighted to have her.

In my view, the remarkable success of these individuals and others is perhaps the strongest evidence that the investing advice and philosophy that I have shared with you in this book is worth following. I sincerely hope that someday I will learn that many of the readers of this book have gone on to make fortunes of their own. You could be one of them.

So my advice to you is to believe in yourself and to act. You can certainly do it too!

The End!

INDEX

"cash flow"